MARIANNE MOORE, Subversive Modernist

MARIANNE MOORE

• • *Subversive Modernist*

by Taffy Martin

University of Texas Press, Austin

First Edition, 1986

Requests for permission to reproduce material from this work
should be sent to Permissions, University of Texas Press, Box 7819,
Austin, Texas 78713-7819.

*The publication of this book was assisted by a grant from the
Andrew W. Mellon Foundation.*

Library of Congress Cataloging-in-Publication Data
Martin, Taffy, 1945–
  Marianne Moore, subversive modernist.
  Bibliography: p.
  Includes index.
  1. Moore, Marianne, 1887–1972—Criticism and
interpretation. 2. Modernism (Literature) I. Title.
PS3525.05616Z695 1986   811'.52   86-4357
ISBN 0-292-73819-6

To the memory of Mary Wynne

Contents

Acknowledgments

THE LATE professor Maurice Beebe, of Temple University and the *Journal of Modern Literature*, read and commented on various drafts of this book so thoroughly and so wisely that he is responsible for much here that is of worth. Patricia Willis, curator of the Marianne Moore collection at the Rosenbach Museum & Library, not only assisted me in my research there but also offered criticism, clues, and boundless good will. Special thanks go to Clive Driver, Moore's literary executor, for use of unpublished material at the Rosenbach. The Woodruff Foundation and the Ossabaw Island Foundation provided financial assistance that gave me some uninterrupted time for writing. Much of my research was made both possible and pleasurable because of the assistance of the staff of Yale University's Beinecke Library. I would also like to acknowledge the cooperation of Isabelle Coupé and André Lardin of the American Library in Paris and of Ruth Etienne and Christiane Peslin of the American Library in Nancy.

The following persons have in countless ways made it possible for me to complete this book. I offer them my heartful thanks and beg the forgiveness of anyone I may have overlooked: Robert Buttel, Robert Detweiler, Rachel DuPlessis, Sally Fitzgerald, Linda and Leo Hamalian, Richard Kennedy, Thomas Kinsella, Trudy Kretchman, Raymond and Camillette Labrunie, Madah Love, Frank Manley, Tom and Joan McLaughlin, Dan O'Hara, Marjorie Perloff, Linda Simon, Elizabeth Stevenson, Diane Wakoski, Linda Wagner, Marion Willis, Philip Yannella.

Finally, I would like to thank my very large and supportive family for waiting and Jean-Pierre Pouzol for understanding.

Introduction

WHEN MARIANNE MOORE died in 1972, having outlived William Carlos Williams, Wallace Stevens, and T. S. Eliot, she had changed the course of American poetry. She had also left her mark on the reading public in an amusing but entirely appropriate way. Almost anyone who has paged through an anthology of poetry or of American literature responds to her name by quoting one of the lines in "Poetry"—"'Imaginary gardens with real toads in them.'" It is amusing and appropriate that people quote Marianne Moore when she is quoting someone else, since their confusion says a good deal about the history of Moore's difficult poetry. Anthology editors find Marianne Moore's poetry useful. Some of her poems illustrate syllabic verse; most are neither too short nor too long for anthologies; and "Poetry" adds an elegantly irreverent touch to collections of poems about poetry. In spite of these frequent appearances, though, Moore's craft distracts her readers. They admire her technique and then miss the excitement, the challenge, and the playful wit of the poems. She becomes a sort of national mascot.

It is easy to see why Moore's poetry appears so frequently in anthologies but difficult to understand why she continues to be known more for her personality or for quotable phrases than for the body of her work or for her importance to other poets. It is also difficult to account for the fact that today Moore receives less critical attention than do her contemporaries, who, in the early decades of the twentieth century, had admired her work for its genius and daring. In spite of recent studies that treat Moore intelligently, the entire history of Moore criticism reveals a pattern of misperception installed as fact. Moore's contemporaries, unlike later readers, recognized both the surface brilliance of her poetry and the subversive nature of her endeavor. Not many years later, academic critics met with frustration when they tried to fit Marianne Moore into the paradigm of high modernism that they were busily developing. Unwilling and unable to ignore Moore's work entirely, that second generation of readers developed a mythic Marianne Moore whose role in the canon of modernism reflected their perceptions of her personality.

Moore's elaborate constructions became defensive, virginal attempts to escape from the chaos in which, they decided, she was distressed to find herself. That myth still exists, in spite of several good recent studies of Moore, and it has come to obscure the poetry itself.

Marianne Moore, Subversive Modernist employs both traditional scholarship and contemporary critical theory in order to recapture the excitement that Moore's contemporaries felt when they encountered her poetry and to reconstruct what I call the subversive side of her work. Moore emerges as a poet who responded to the twentieth century with humorous irony and aggressive optimism. Her blend of ideas was unique in its time. She was both at the center of twentieth-century modernism and at its outer limits. She was a misfit in her puritanical beliefs, but she was just as much a misfit in the heretical quality of her personal version of twentieth-century modernism.

It would be an all-encompassing task to construct yet one more definition of modernism. Virginia Woolf's pioneering essays "Mr. Bennet and Mrs. Brown" and "The Leaning Tower" set the question of modernism in perspective. Later studies, such as Maurice Beebe's *Ivory Towers and Sacred Founts,* turn modernism into an institution, complete with definitions and counter arguments. Indeed, the latest contributions to the now considerable mountain of criticism define modernism in terms of its wayward but often favored child, postmodernism. Just as no one tries to pretend that either of these terms is satisfactory, let alone melodious, no one expects to find general agreement about what these awkward words mean. Short of inventing an entirely new language, however, the concepts of modernism and postmodernism are essential to any discussion of Marianne Moore. She was a full-fledged but subversive modernist whose treatment of twentieth-century experience undermines the outward calm so essential to modernism as it is usually defined. She thus anticipates the jagged confusion that postmodernists proposed as a more appropriate response to contemporary experience.

Twentieth-century modernism was, as literary critics sometimes forget, not just an international but also an interdisciplinary phenomenon. Nevertheless, for many American writers and for the American practical critics who helped to establish their reputations, modernism was a literary response to the challenge of living in the inhospitable world of the twentieth century. Art—literary art in particular—offered a refuge from the threat of overwhelming chaos. Stasis, frozen images, and imposed order were the basis of this literary modernism. Thus, T. S. Eliot's attempt to make sense out of James Joyce's portrait of a chaotic, senseless, or threatening Dublin becomes the academic critic's touchstone. Classic myth imposed upon that frightful scene freezes it, nullifies its inherent danger, and makes it—the city having given way to the novel—suitable for admiration as a work of art. Postmodernism sets out to topple this possibility of repose. It replaces stasis and frozen images with gaps and instabilities.

Anxious to escape from the perceived barbaric uncivility of their non-European origins, many American writers migrated toward what they saw as the real center of modernism and became expatriates. Eliot eventually became a British citizen. Pound wandered restlessly before settling in Italy. H. D. and Mina Loy, while nowhere near as dogmatic as their male counterparts, also took the expatriate road and embraced to varying degrees European modernism. But not all writers saw modernism as an essentially European affair. There were American writers just as determined to "stay put" and find modernism at home as there were those anxious to leave, and this "stay put" version is the modernism which Moore aligned herself with and then subverted. The idea of a distinctively American modernism is not a new one. Hugh Kenner properly describes the symbiosis between Americans and their machines, but American writers in the early decades of the twentieth century recognized the two-way relationship as well. There were as many artist-proponents of mechanization and mass production as there were aesthetic warriors against it. Marcel Duchamp's "compositions" attempted to undermine any critic ready to identify yet one more iconic escape from the rubble of wordly imperfection.

Parallel to this fascination with the machine was American modernism's determination to divest itself of the burden of the past—not just nineteenth-century romanticism, but European and British assumptions, beliefs, and mannerisms. These writers insisted on portraying the experience of living, writing, or otherwise making art in the United States in the twentieth century. Marianne Moore and William Carlos Williams were the chief poets among the dogmatically American modernists, and some of their early writings are so cross-referential that their texts become inextricably intertwined. Among the components of their version of American modernism were attention to ordinary objects rather than "poetic" subjects and a relentless search for an illusive concept—"the American idiom." Poets as well as critics have since realized that there is no such thing as *the* American idiom; but the poetry that Moore, Williams, and others wrote in an attempt to capture that idiom has left its indisputable mark on twentieth-century poetry.

But in spite of their early accord, the critical fortunes of Moore and Williams have diverged. Williams, of course, moved restlessly toward longer lines and longer poems. His success in having captured that illusive American idiom might be measured by the comments of such Americans-by-adoption as Thomas Kinsella and Denise Levertov. Each claims that reading Williams, more so than moving to and living in the

United States, was the key experience in gaining a new sense of language and poetic idiom. Williams was also the chief figure for and the chief influence on the entire branch of contemporary poetry that has come to be known as postmodern or Black Mountain poetry. Moore, of course, did not develop along those same lines. Furthermore, her constant process of revision and deletion makes it nearly impossible to chart a single line of development in her style. Poems double back upon one another and result in her being condemned as fussy. The criticism that has prevailed relegates Moore to the domain of static and iconic European modernism. Her craft and her precision become defensive barriers against the chaos around her. But, in fact, just the opposite is true. Moore maintained her allegiance to both the machine-fascinated and idiom-searching school of American modernism. Out of those interests and because of her undeniable talent for and love of precision, Moore created an entire body of work that anticipates not only postmodern literature but related manifestations of postmodernism as well.

Moore's subversion of the stifling parts of European modernism and the strain of American modernism that modeled itself on European modernism—the insistence that art was art by virtue of and in direct relation to its escape from life—is not nearly so manic as Yossarian's mad ravings in Joseph Heller's *Catch 22*, but her patterning bears the marks of other artists whose works have become reference points for postmodernism. Rather than the pioneering but still recognizably musical compositions of Aaron Copland, Moore's quotation-littered poems make one think of John Cage's music, in which artificial time constraints and found sounds replace traditional phrasing. Moore's attention to curious objects, her refusal to set most poems into a recognizable narrative, and her nearly too startling metaphors become not precious mannerisms but postmodern credentials when they appear in Frank O'Hara's poems. And Moore's carefully constructed and just as carefully fractured and interrupted compositions resemble the music of Steve Reich and Philip Glass and the talking dances of Trisha Brown. Moore's poems have often been compared to collage, but they resemble more specifically Joseph Cornell's boxes. Accuracy, patterning, and repetition are essential tools of the postmodern musicians, dancers, and visual artists whose work Moore anticipates. Their responses to and their interpretations of life in the twentieth century are inclusive rather than defensive or escapist, just as Marianne Moore's were. They acknowledge and exploit the machine, which was so important to Moore and her fellow American modernists, and they do so within their own versions of the American idiom. Whether these similarities prove, as some critics have always argued, that postmodernism does not really exist, that it is merely a continuation of modernism (which was, after all, a continuation of romanticism), is not the question here. Nevertheless, this attempt to establish a context for the terms modernism and postmodernism should provide a starting point for reading Moore's work and understanding the way in which she plays within, manages to escape from, subverts, and thus redefines American modernism.

Whether in personal comments, critical essays, or individual poems, Moore employed scientifically accurate observation to record sensuous details and to convey her idiosyncratic interpretation of American modernism. Thus, at the very height of modernist concern with fragmentation and disorder, Moore assumes a dialectical stance and subverts even the possibility of its synthesis. Instead, she acknowledges and enacts irresolvable multiplicity by denying chronological order, by incorporating fragmentary quotations into her own work, and finally by questioning the stability of her medium, language. In the process of writing such essays and poems, Moore undermines established literary tradition. Moore's break with nineteenth-century romanticism was decisive. Her response was not a grand design but a curious combination of wit, tenacity, impressionability, and power. Her work is a continuous fictive discourse that replaces the lyre of traditional poetry with everyday words and with heretical ideas about language itself.

Part One of this book examines three neglected aspects of Moore's work: her careful preparation for a career as a poet, her early prose essays, and her editorship of *The Dial*. These explorations lead to a fuller awareness of Moore's strange complexities and contradictions. Part Two builds upon this information and examines Moore's poetry, her concept of imaginative creation, and its relationship to that of her fellow poets. Moore admits that an intractable mind has "its own ax to grind," and uses her poetry as an ax both to expose and to deconstruct the literary assumptions of high modernism. In their place, she offers an amused response to the questions that plagued so many modernist writers.

Chapter 1 develops a portrait of Marianne Moore as a highly motivated and deliberately self-conscious young woman, determined to succeed as a writer. That poet, like the versions of "Poetry" that Moore either tucked away in her notes or banished to a pile of discarded manuscripts, rests behind the facade which, curiously enough, Moore herself had developed. Moore's unpublished correspondence, her reading notebooks, her workbooks, and several romans à clef portraying Moore help to correct the lopsided impression that she was little more than a teetotaling, feminine mascot for the bohemian Greenwich Village writers who confronted modernism singlehandedly.

Chapter 2 builds upon the knowledge of Moore's determination and examines her early prose essays in order to explore and to reconstruct Moore's idiosyncratic creative process. It becomes clear that her peculiar use of quotation and her subtly imitative form developed out of a life-long habit of collecting, recording, and indexing quotations. Moore deliberately blurred the chronology and sometimes the identity of those quotations in order to enact rather than shy away from the complexity of her subject. The stance is assertive rather than defensive. The essays also account for Moore's ability to embrace the fragmentation that so many modernist writers tried to diminish and control.

The early essays develop the critical principles that Moore later employed in selecting poetry, fiction, and criticism for *The Dial*. Chapter 3 shows that, as editor of the most influential magazine of the 1920s, Moore reversed the magazine's patrician attempt to tame the rough edges and resolve the contradictions inherent in the twentieth century. Moore's monthly editorial, "Comment," demonstrates her ironic optimism, and the column becomes her definition of American modernism, one that anticipates Michel Foucault's archaeological, antidynastic view of history as a series of discontinuous, radical breaks.

Part Two turns to Moore's poetry and builds upon the patterns of attention and taste that emerged in Part One. Moore's determined optimism and subversive approach influence her treatment of imaginative creation and dictate the curious method of her poetry. What some critics see as fastidious or docile behavior becomes a calculated part of her creative design. Part Two also shows how contemporary critical theory—particularly deconstruction—helps to define Moore's private discourse. I avoid treating Moore's poetry chronologically and have not forced the poems into a seamless critical fiction. Thus, while I pay close attention to individual works, making use of the valuable lesson of New Criticism, I look primarily at Moore's contribution to and perception of American modernism. Comparing Moore's work to that of her contemporaries makes her opposition to established tradition even clearer.

Chapter 4 explores the ways in which Moore uses imaginative creation to construct her own negatively capable fiction. She admits the insufficiency of her fictive constructs and argues for radical ambiguity and indeterminacy as positive alternatives. In doing so, Moore again anticipates postmodern thought. Indeterminacy and radical ambiguity affect even the shape of Moore's poetry, and Chapter 5 examines the ways in which this happens. Moore leads her readers to expect traditional images, solutions, and verbal structures; but she gives them images that dissolve, epigrammatic endings that solve nothing, and quotations that disfigure rather than preserve speech.

The concluding chapter returns to the portrait begun in the first chapter and completes the picture of the poet behind the myth of Marianne Moore. The determined spirit within her poetry refuses to submit to traditional methods of interpretation and does not reveal a grand design that lends itself to ultimate solutions. Moore's ongoing private discourse must be taken on its own terms.

Just as Moore disfigures the quotations residing within her poems and subverts the stability of both spoken and written language, she constructs her own critical impasse and then shows how to dismantle it. Her clue is the smile, which appears as humorous irony in her essays and editorial decisions. In the poetry, Moore's smile acknowledges that "we do not admire what we cannot understand," but it also keeps alive the possibility of genuine engagement with what we do not understand. A series of photographs, which Moore appears to have commissioned just after she had moved to New York, illustrates the puzzle of Marianne Moore and suggests the interpretation she wants her readers to make. Most of the photographs are formal studio shots that depict an inscrutable young woman dressed in a tailored suit and a white shirt. Her soft hair, small but determined chin, and warm eyes do little to counteract the severe tone and composition of the portraits. Another photograph does that quite well. In it, Moore wears similar clothing but stands outdoors in front of a large brownstone house, her arm nonchalantly draped over the neck of a small pony. In that picture alone, Moore is smiling. That smile pervades Moore's work and bespeaks courage, determination, intelligence, and privacy. Like those more formal portraits, Moore's poetry occasionally seems overdetermined and severe. Sometimes it is. But Moore tempers that austerity with a smile—often ironic, just as often genuinely playful—and goes on to create her own private music.

PART ONE ▪ "So Much Color"

wide-eyed and watchful
and entirely careless
of what was done or thought
by the beholders
—Virginia Woolf
  "Time Passes," *To the Lighthouse*

1 · Portrait of a Writing Master

AMONG THE MANY animals found in Marianne Moore's poetry, perhaps the most surprising is a dragon. Even more surprising is Moore's uncharacteristically straightforward admission that she would like to be a dragon. That dragon, "of silkworm size or immense" or perhaps "almost invisible," would be, Moore claims, a "Felicitous phenomenon." The dragon also offers valuable insight into the person behind the tame exterior that Marianne Moore constructed by means of her poetry. As the centennial of Moore's birth approaches and critics begin to reassess her work, the appropriateness of that dragon becomes clear. Unlike the unicorn—equally fabulous but shrouded in mystery and symbolic of meditative companionship—the dragon is a fighter, a serpent, and in mythic terms an insatiable warrior. It is surprising, therefore, that Moore's critics often treat her as a decorative oddity rather than as an active and perhaps even dangerous force. To a great extent, the blame for this misperception lies with Moore herself.

Establishing the origin of the myth of Marianne Moore and tracing the reification and subsequent recognition of that myth are thus the starting points of this chapter. Moore's poetry itself is the source of the myth; New Criticism is the agent of its installation as fact. Moore herself provides the evidence that exposes and then counteracts the myth. The first part of this evidence is her own private papers and letters, which have only recently been made available. They reveal Moore's methodical ambition and unshakable determination and show that her discipline was tempered by humorous irony. The portraits drawn by Moore's friends in their memoirs of the period reinforce this complex image. After exploring the myth of Marianne Moore and then taking into account Moore's own evidence and the testimony of her friends, one can begin to see beyond that myth and read her poetry more fully. This chapter then concludes by examining several Moore poems whose subject is defensive armoring but whose speaker is as fearless a warrior as that of her own mythic dream, the dragon. "The Pangolin" shows that an inner drive for privacy and equanimity rather than fearful withdrawal

attracts one to protective disguise. The speaker of "Melancthon" luxuri-
ates in the sensuous privacy of his impenetrability. "Marriage" displays
bitter cynicism toward its subject, concentrating on the blindness of its
participants and the danger of hiding behind easy assumptions about
that institution. "The Octopus" counteracts that mood by arguing that
complexity and incomprehensibility can be enjoyable on their own
terms. Moore goes on to make that positive approach her tool for exploring the nature of poetry and even the efficacy of the written word.

While the opening lines of "The Pangolin," "Another armored animal," [1] are surely self-parody, there is ample evidence throughout Moore's
poetry to support the opposing readings that find Moore, of necessity,
hiding behind a defensive, protective covering. In "The Fish" brittle
scales turn invasive light back upon itself. In "Melancthon" thick skin
serves as an impermeable barrier. In "The Steeple-Jack" the geometry of
Moore's frozen seaside scene seems impervious. The perfection of her
landscape protects the town's residents from any suggestion of danger.
The examples are innumerable, but the poems are, of course, not quite
so simple. Moore's first critics recognized the extent to which she tried to
emphasize rather than diminish contradiction, and much recent criticism is returning to that point of view.

Nevertheless, at least one ongoing perception of Marianne Moore fails
to recognize Moore's complexity and the depth of her deliberate ambiguity. This misperception is to a large extent the result of the popular image
of Marianne Moore—one which she herself constructed. Based in fact,
the image gains power from the contrast between Moore's experimental
poetry and her extraordinarily ordinary life. It is, in fact, Moore's intention to be private and ordinary that distinguishes her idiosyncracies from
the self-conscious affectation of T. S. Eliot's morning-coat formality, from
Ezra Pound's cultivated outlandishness, and even more so from the many
liberated ladies of Greenwich Village. Kenneth Burke attributes the
incongruity, in part, to Moore's extraordinary intelligence and to her
nearly obsessive attention to detail. On occasion, he reports, she would
be nearly overcome by the visual stimuli in a museum. Well aware of this
unusual trait, Moore tried, Burke says, to diminish an outsider's perception of her impressionability and sensitivity. "She tried so hard to be
ordinary that she became even more extraordinary." [2]

Moore also stood apart from her contemporaries in her everyday life.
The details of Moore's living arrangements are so ordinary that she
seems almost a nineteenth-century anachronism in the setting of Greenwich Village in the 1920s. Following her graduation from Bryn Mawr
College, Moore lived with her mother until Mrs. Moore's death in 1947.
This fact, combined with Moore's formal speech and manner, puzzled
and even irritated Moore's friends. Memoirs of the period record Moore's

reserve so persuasively that subsequent readers of those memoirs have created a myth out of the person and have begun, unlike her contemporaries, to read the poetry in terms of the myth. This process, especially when it is unconscious, works as a disservice to Moore's work and to her critical reputation.

An archaeological tour of the history of Moore criticism helps to trace the progress of the myth. One sees that more and more over the years, critics read the poetry in terms of Moore's public image. Recent studies have begun to reverse that trend. Uninfluenced by what was to become the dogma of New Criticism, Moore's contemporaries recognized her quaint manner and habits but did not incorporate those qualities into critical readings of her work. They admired the poetry and envied Moore's erudition. In subsequent years, however, Moore's mannerisms came to influence her critics. This occurs, ironically, just at the time when those very critics began arguing for rigorously analytical treatments of literature. R. P. Blackmur appears to be a turning point. In 1935 he insisted upon an approach that "treats of nothing in literature except in its capacity of reduction to literary fact."[3] "In making a formal approach to Marianne Moore," he explains, one needs "special terms and special adjustments to meet the texture and pattern of the poems."[4] Blackmur's treatment of Moore is careful and perceptive, but his reading of "Marriage" violates his own critical principles. Calling it a poem "never concerned with either love or lust" (84), he contends that "no poet has been so chaste" (85). When Blackmur goes on to explain that Moore's work presents a "special chastity aside from the flesh," he reveals a predisposition toward her work that results in a circular condemnation of her poetry. "In Miss Moore," according to Blackmur, "life is remote . . . and everything is done to keep it remote" (85). This sensibility "predicted her poetic method; and the defect of her method, in its turn, only represents the idiosyncrasy of her sensibility: that it, like its subject matter, constitutes the perfection of standing aside" (86).

Later critics move farther away from the core of Moore's poetry and concentrate instead on the ways in which the poetry fails to satisfy their own criteria for good modernist poetry. John Crowe Ransom found her "free verse" to have "little formal clarity" and called it "a break in the poetic style book that has done service for so long."[5] Missing the excitement of Moore's deliberate break with the "stylebook" of modernism and the importance of that break, Ransom attempts merely to "identify the precise moment of her discontinuity and so at least reduce it to a minimum" (136). Like Blackmur, Ransom then assigns Moore's work to second-class status and labels it "the handsomest consequence . . . of the imagist cult of thirty years ago" (136).

Much the same is true for studies that followed Ransom's and found

Moore's poetry to be "cautious and cautionary . . . essentially uncommitted,"[6] "a gesture of fastidiousness,"[7] "not especially modern, not of the twentieth century,"[8] and the tame product of "the orderly world of 'benevolent conclusiveness' that Moore feels safest in."[9] The image of Moore as a quaint aberration has also produced readings that inexplicably contradict themselves. In *Homemade World,* Hugh Kenner places Moore, along with Pound, Williams, Stevens, Hemingway, Fitzgerald, and Zukofsky, into the select group of writers who "rethought and altered, perhaps permanently, the novel and especially the poem."[10] But in describing what he imagines to be Moore's specific contribution, Kenner sees her as little more than a twentieth-century amanuensis. Calling Moore the poet of the typewriter, Kenner explains that "we discern Miss Moore being a librarian, an editor, a teacher of typewriting: locating fragments already printed; picking and choosing; making, letter by letter, neat pages" (98).

Recent critics, to be discussed more fully in later chapters, are just now rejecting these readings. Feminist critics have begun to champion Moore as an independent spirit, but she does not fit easily into standard feminist readings. In most studies, Moore receives only token mention as a twentieth-century modernist whose chief accomplishment is her mastery of quotable quotations. Suzanne Juhasz, in *Modern American Poetry by Women,* goes much farther by championing Moore as one of the few giants of American poetry. Juhasz, however, goes on to lament Moore's severely curtailed if not nonexistent romantic life. Juhasz feels that the absence of sexual relationships limits the range of Moore's poetry. In addition to feminists, critical theorists have turned to Moore's work and recognized her complex designs as playful tools. Geoffrey Hartmann pairs Moore with Hegel and Derrida; Frank Lentricchia treats Moore's poetry more fully. In doing so, he uses her as a motif for discussing other modern poets. Marjorie Perloff includes Moore in her study of the relationship between early William Carlos Williams and contemporary avant-garde poetry. These recent studies, whether by feminists, critical theorists, or postmodernists, reject the popular image of Moore and instead discover ways in which Marianne Moore substantiates their own theories.

Full-length studies of Moore, while less polemical in their approach, continue to turn away from the myth of Marianne Moore. Laurence Stapleton's *The Poet's Advance* emphasizes Moore's wit and takes account of her private papers. Bonnie Costello's *Imaginary Possessions* goes on to develop a thorough reading of Moore's chief images. Moore's unpublished notebooks lead Costello to some of the fullest readings of Moore's poetry that have yet been published. Moore, the timid, frightened lady in the black hat, does not exist for Costello. She has been replaced by a poet whose most persuasive images are those of combat and warfare.

While it is refreshing to see that the myth has been discarded as useless by some of Moore's critics and has been put aside in favor of more timely appropriations by theoretical critics, it is nonetheless necessary to look at the evidence Moore herself provided to engender the myth. It quickly becomes clear that control is indeed the subject of Moore's poetry. Many critics automatically see this interest as hermetic and unfortunate. In fact, the control is the product of Moore's limitless ambition, as controlled and controlling as the "spruce cone regularity" that she admired in the armored scales of "The Pangolin." But by filtering daily experience and personal circumstance through the enabling straightjacket of her control, Moore created a poetry as personal and emotional as it sometimes seems distant. Moore's poems frequently glorify passionate intensity and seek out chaos and danger. Her pangolin *is* another armored animal, but it is one with "everlasting vigor, / power to grow." The pangolin thus becomes one version of "the self, the being we call human, writing- / master to this world" (119).

Like a dutiful writing master, Moore meticulously documented her progress toward becoming one. Her record of that progress now provides the evidence for an alternate view of the poet herself. Moore was a voracious reader and a dedicated record keeper. She saved family letters, reading and appointment notebooks, letters from acquaintances, and carbon copies of her responses to those letters, as well as manuscripts and drafts of her published and unpublished work and even records of her revisions of published work. This material forms a remarkably detailed and complete record of Moore's intellectual and professional development, particularly for the early years of her career. During that time, Moore prepared herself to be both a critic and a poet. She considered everything, regardless of source or chronology, potentially appropriate material for her writing. The manuscripts document her breadth of reference and her use of fragmentary quotations, but more importantly they show that these practices were lifelong habits, part of her conscious preparation for a public career.

Moore's habit of reading and recording grew out of a longstanding family habit of voluminous letter writing. Thus, the documentation of Marianne Moore's adult life begins to emerge in a remarkable series of letters written between 1905 and 1909, while Moore was a student at Bryn Mawr College. A round of letters began several times a week with a letter from Mrs. Moore at her home in Carlisle, Pennsylvania. She sent it to Moore's brother, Warner, who read it, sometimes wrote one of his own, and sent both to Marianne at Bryn Mawr. Moore then wrote a letter and sent all three back to Carlisle. Although the series did not always progress in this manner, most of the letters still exist and provide a detailed record of the family during this period. In them, the family members address one another by pet names, many of them drawn from *The Wind in the Willows*. Mrs. Moore was Bunny Fawn or Mole, Warner was Badger, and Marianne, Mice or Rat. The names suggest a playful intimacy, and the letters occasionally engage in lighthearted jesting. More frequently, however, they are characterized by Mrs. Moore's attempts to organize her children's lives and to encourage them to be ambitious. In November 1908, during Moore's senior year, Mrs. Moore wrote her daughter that in spite of the financial struggle Marianne's education represented, "the thing all important this year in regard to Bryn Mawr is that you get the most out of it—that it will yield intellectually and socially." [11] Apparently Moore agreed wholeheartedly. In a letter written on her twenty-first birthday, Moore records—with the attention to detail that would characterize much of her later work and with a curious dispassion—just how she was progressing in her schoolwork. [12] After thanking the family for their birthday gifts—a skirt, a box of figs, and a book of Yeats's poetry—she describes her activities for the week. In addition to studying, playing hockey, and attending a play that her classmates had produced, Moore was planning for the future. Her ideas reveal both the discipline and the enthusiasm that would characterize all of her later work. The control of the writing master is already visible: "Writing is too much in line with my natural excesses for me to experiment with it ad libitum so I decided to waive pence and glory and resign from the *Tip* [Bryn Mawr's literary magazine]—as a reward of merit, if I get good marks in February, I shall ask to be let into the imitative writing course. They read all the nineteenth-century books and criticize as much as they write which I think I should like." Moore concludes the letter with her account of a sermon she had heard that day—a Tuesday—at church: "An Episcopalian from East Orange preached. He said discouragement was egotism."

Moore seems to have taken this message to heart. The pattern of hard work and academic achievement that her mother had encouraged and that Marianne Moore records in the college letters continued to be a part of her life. After graduating from Bryn Mawr, Moore returned to Carlisle, where she attended Carlisle Community College and later taught at the United States Industrial Indian School there. During that period, Moore also continued her education on her own. She recorded much of the process in a form less public and conscious than the letters, which were always aware of an audience, even though of only two people.

Beginning in 1916, just after Moore had published her first poems in *Poetry* and *The Egoist*, she began keeping a series of reading and conversation notebooks, which she continued throughout her life. They supplement the picture of Moore's industry and meticulous record keeping, and they reveal a good bit about her creative method. Most importantly, as a part of Moore's intellectual biography, they show that her idiosyncratic interests were a private matter rather than a public affectation. Much like commonplace books, the notebooks contain quotations from Moore's reading and almost no comments of her own. Far from being strictly literary, Moore's sources range from Bertrand Russell's *Introduction to Mathematical Philosophy* and critical studies of contemporary authors to museum catalogues, *Vogue* magazine, and *Boy's Life*. She covered nearly every inch of the notebooks in microscopic handwriting, indicating the source and often the page number of every reference. But the most remarkable feature of these notebooks is Moore's inclusion at the end of each volume of a complete index according to the author, title, and subject of her entries.

It is impossible to determine whether Moore knew how she would eventually use these indexes in composing poems, but they are now valuable for what they show not only about the almost incredible range of her interests but also about her creative method. Moore's notebooks contain numerous references to the animals that appear throughout the poetry. In the index to her first reading notebook, for instance, under the heading "animals" she lists "albino snakes, black bear, blacks and wrens at Pan, crocodiles in Palestine, crows, frigate birds, giraffe, grizzly bear, elephants," and a number of other animals. In composing poems, she used her notes for finding quotations, probably by relying first on memory and then on a notebook's index. Thus, one poem might contain quotations that she had discovered and recorded on several occasions, often years apart. What caught Moore's attention varied from a single vivid image or a point of information, such as a passage from Darwin's *Variations of Plants and Animals under Domestication*, to a passage on any subject that caught Moore's eye because of its phrasing or humor. This appreciation of phrasing was also the case with Moore's conversation notebooks, which were collections of quotations, often by Moore's mother but just as frequently phrases from an exchange overheard by chance in public. In both instances, Moore kept the records for her own pleasure and information. The practice becomes another indication of the private side of Moore's industry and the methodical nature of her work.

A more public side of Moore's ambition emerged when she traveled to New York to meet some of the young writers who were living there. Once again she preserved a careful record of her endeavor, this time in a series of letters to her brother. First Moore outlined her preparations for the undertaking. A series of three letters then recounts every detail of the visit, calling it her "Sojourn in the Whale." Parts of the first letter, in which Moore writes that she has "collected addresses by the thousands," sound as though they had been written by an impressionable adolescent more concerned with her present appearance than her plans for the future: "I have an airdale coat and I'm goan [sic] to New York on Monday. . . . It's a simple coat, black with blue and green stripes, . . . it has leather buttons about the size of a buckeye, made of plaited leather down the front and a full cut of sleeve and collar. It is finished with catchstitching inside and the finest quality of black satin." [13] In contrast to the first letter, Moore's account of her stay, written after she had returned to Carlisle, displays self-confidence and energetic drive as well as exuberance. She describes, for instance, how Alfred Kreymborg dressed and what he and his wife served her for dinner. But she also describes every detail of her visit to Alfred Steiglitz's studio and the conversations she and Kreymborg had about encouraging new writers to send their poetry to his magazine, *Others*. [14] It is clear that the trip gave Moore confidence that she would be able to succeed as a writer. A note Moore added to one of Mrs. Moore's letters to Warner shows that she was interested in writing criticism:

> I feel I can get a job with the [Philadelphia] *Ledger* . . . by my concentrated and cumulative exertions, am just as sure of getting it as I am of eating, if I could only see them. I am doing a couple of sample reviews. . . . and what with my poems of a critical trend in *The Egoist* and *Poetry* and *Others* and *Contemporary Verse* and my Indian experience, I should certainly extort the position. I am prepared to review poetry, fiction, art or theology. Music and sport and dancing are the only things I am afraid to tackle. [15]

Instead of working as a reviewer, Moore continued to write poetry and to plan for her future. In 1916, she moved with her mother to Chatham, New Jersey, where her brother had been appointed minister at a Presbyterian church. Following shortly after Moore's exploratory sojourn, the move was clearly part of her design for a career as a poet and a critic. Only twenty-five miles from New York, Chatham offered relatively easy access to the emerging literary and artistic circles there without the radical change that a move to New York would have presented. One of Moore's letters to H. D., written shortly after Moore's move to New Jersey, displays a similar combination of ambition and cautious reserve: "I should like to try a comparison of George Moore and Fielding; also one of Knut Hamsun and Carlyle and one of Wallace Stevens and Compton Mackenzie. I am very much interested, also, in William [Carlos] Williams' work, but I am a little afraid to undertake a criticism of it. I feel that I have not seen enough of it to justify my writing one." [16]

The ambition and caution, determination and reserve, frivolity and meticulous attention to detail that appear here, in Moore's other early letters, and in her notebooks continued throughout her life and helped to produce the work that brought her critical recognition. Just as frequently, these personality traits confounded those who met her. Out of the contrast between her astonishing work and her eccentric personality grew confused amusement, then myth, and eventually misperception.

Moore's friendship with William Williams, as she insisted upon calling the poet for many years, represents the first stage of the process. The two admired each other's work and soon became close friends. But Williams was unable to break through Moore's reserve. Instead, the two seem to have enjoyed and cultivated their differences. From the first, Williams enjoyed playing the bohemian tempter to Moore's reserve. He once promised to drink only "sacramental wine" if Moore would attend a party with the "crowd" in which, he said, she seemed both in and out of place, like a red berry hanging to a jaded rosebush.[17] True to her adopted role and in her best documentary style, Moore answered, typing a carbon of her response on the verso of Williams's letter. She said that she knew her reserved manner kept her at the fringe of the Greenwich Village crowd but felt no discomfort with that standing, since "I cannot feel sorry for the red berry when the bush is so full of sap."

This exchange shows that Moore both assented to and participated in the image that Williams and many of his friends had constructed. For instance, Moore is invariably remembered for appearing in Alfred Kreymborg's *Troubadour* as the endearing baseball fan who surprised Williams and Kreymborg by her knowledge of the game. That, however, was only part of the portrayal. Kreymborg had also described Moore as "an astonishing person with Titian hair, a brilliant complexion and a mellifluous flow of polysyllables which held every man in awe."[18] He added that what many of their Village friends "lacked in intellectual ability was freely and consciously supplied by her [and] her familiarity with books on every conceivable subject astonished them" (186–87).

Robert McAlmon's portrait of Moore in his roman à clef *Post Adolescence* also seems to approach caricature, especially in the most commonly excerpted passages, which make particular note of Moore's closeness to her mother. However, Moore's portrait deserves careful attention since it turns out to be the most flattering one in the book and shows why Moore's friends thought of her as they did. McAlmon presents a complex Marianne Moore who startled her companions more by her intelligence and productivity than by her conventional or even eccentric mannerisms. The novel follows the aimless wanderings of Peter (McAlmon), who, like many of his friends, wanted mainly to "dance, sing, paint, copulate, eat, sleep, and finally die."[19] He portrays Vera St. Vitus

(Edna St. Vincent Millay) as "a nice girl [who] doesn't use her head" (92) and Gusta Rolph (Mina Loy) as "a dancer," notable chiefly for her "dandruff-tossing, eye-glistening semitic vivacity" (2–3). In contrast to these limited portrayals, Martha Wullus (Marianne Moore) appears in the novel's penultimate chapter as a "rather quaint" person, complex and initially not easily likeable. "She thinks anything, disapproves of little, for other people, and is a churchgoing, cerebralizing moralist who observes sabbath day strictly, herself." Peter "can't quite understand why with a mind like hers agnosticism hasn't eaten into her a little" and thinks that he ought to be "bored to death with Martha Wullus." He isn't, though, because he "can't get her angle." Peter's friend, Brander Ogden (Marsden Hartley), is hardly more encouraging, calling her a "quaint idea rather than a real human being." Peter agrees, adding that it is probably "best for her to be only an idea, too, seeing that ideas is about all she'll ever have out of life." Thus, when Peter, Brander, and Gusta decide to call on Martha and her mother at their Greenwich Village basement apartment, it is no surprise that Martha speaks too formally for the comfort of her guests. "O good day and how have all of you been, you Miss Rolph, particularly? I've so wanted to have a conversation with you because of what I've heard about your work" (104).

The visit turns out to be a dismal one during which Martha's ever-present mother "drawled out her observations, making distinctions of her exact meaning with a too careful honesty that had its limitations." Martha, in her world of ideas, worries that her work at the library keeps her from "my work, the real kind I'm wanting to do." Gusta refuses to believe this and all but accuses Martha of success. "Bother your paid work. You observe things too uniquely to let any paid job interfere with your writing. Though I presume you believe in self-discipline and duty more than some of us do." The young guests plan an escape and take Martha with them to a "dingy little bohemian cafe." In the cafe, Martha continues to speak in her elaborately formal sentences, this time on the subject of self-discipline. She admits that finding time to work is difficult but shows that she has consciously turned that struggle into an advantage. "It's restraining oneself in the midst of annoyances to which one is subjected that toughens the muscles. Wildness in itself is an attractive quality, but it fails to take into account the question of attrition and attrition is inevitable." Certainly no product of attrition, Martha describes her writing with steadfast conviction. "I'm telling you the truth when I say that if I had all the time in the world I should not write anything important to myself for some years. In order to work as I should have to, I should like to look into certain things and make up my mind with regard to the relevance, or irrelevance, of certain other things. That may be hard for you to realize, but it is quite true, and I have, I think, an intuition as to how I am to succeed if I do succeed" (104–119). The novel ends with Peter's self-indulgent disillusionment, made all the more painful by his reflections upon Martha's confident intuition of success.

The accuracy with which McAlmon captured the rhythm of Moore's speech and her "intuition" of success reflects her real-life comments to him on the subject. In fact, his portrayal of Moore turns out to be almost pure documentation. In 1921, three years before McAlmon published *Post Adolescence*, he had married Bryher (Winifred Ellerman) on short notice and much to the dismay of many of their friends. Williams exploits the event in his *Autobiography*, alluding to Bryher's lesbian relationship with H. D.; but Moore was unhappy for entirely different reasons. On one level, she disapproved of the suddenness of the marriage and wrote McAlmon saying so. McAlmon tried to answer Moore's criticism by insisting that he had married Bryher to rescue her from the domination of her parents and thereby give her the freedom that Americans had. He also insisted that marriage was a private affair, adding that as a sign of her independence Bryher was keeping her own name.[20] Not at all persuaded by McAlmon's excuses, Moore answered that such symbols were meaningless. "It is very nice of you to accord a woman as much freedom as she might care to have but I think a woman's keeping her own name seems like clutching at the last straw of self-identification."[21] For Moore, self-identification would grow out of her work rather than a romance. She wanted success as a writer and believed that marriage, or any relationship, would distract a woman's attention away from her creative work. She explained this in a subsequent letter to Bryher and added that instead Bryn Mawr "gave me security in my determination to have what I want."[22]

Thus, like the contradiction that Moore so arrogantly included in her poetry, she presents a contradiction herself. Lover of order and Dürer-like precision, she often appears docile or retiring. But beneath and because of that demeanor lies deepest feeling and unshakable determination. Both sides of the personality appear throughout Moore's work, and she invites her readers to share in the delight that this apparent puzzle presents. In "Melancthon" her thick-skinned elephant is impervious to arrows and other unwanted intrusions, but it also enjoys the sensual experience of immersing itself in the mud. "An Octopus" praises "neatness of finish" and "relentless accuracy" but within the same stanza undermines that praise by making the dangerous unpredictability of the glacier even more appealing. The speaker of "Marriage," so able to dismiss "This institution, . . . out of respect for which / one says one need not change one's mind," also acknowledges the power of the sexual passion that so controlled and confused the married people of the poem.

This two-sided approach appears throughout Moore's poetry, but the new insights drawn from Moore's private papers make it possible to look at how consistently she develops contrasting points of view within each poem. She delights not in introducing and then resolving tensions but in emphasizing the delightful impossibility of their resolution. This is particularly true in "The Steeple-Jack," which opened Moore's 1935 *Selected Poems* and all subsequent collections of her work. The poem is a tangle of brilliant images warning that surface appearances may be misleading. Once again, some new, unpublished material points toward Moore's love of confusion. Her response to a query about the setting of the poem is informative, but she seems to have enjoyed stopping short of solving the riddle completely:

C. J. Poole was a Brooklyn steeple-jack who worked on the various high buildings and steeples and had his name on the sidewalk danger sign, warning passersby to keep clear of ropes and grapnels on the sidewalk. He was repairing the steeple of the Lafayette Avenue Presbyterian Church, the steeple was finally considered infirm and was replaced by 4 Gothic points.

Dürer was interested in the whales he saw near Amsterdam; and eight whales were stranded in Brooklyn Bay.** I had in mind both Brooklyn and various New England seacoast towns I had visited.

■   ■   ■   ■   ■

**Or perhaps it was near Sheepshead Bay. I have somewhere a newspaper clipping about the whales attracting sightsee-ers.[23]

Moore offers information but not answers, details which "fail" to solve the puzzle. The letter thus intensifies rather than diminishes the unsettling complexities of the poem.

"The Steeple-Jack" itself includes a series of surprising alterations of deliberately set expectations, possible chiefly because of Moore's skillful use of a complex syllabic structure rather than traditional rhythmic line divisions. "Flock" in the second stanza becomes a verb, not a noun, as the preceding words had led us to expect, and "sea-" in the fourth stanza becomes "sea-side flowers." Even more insistently, the narrative itself is unsettling. The poem opens with a stanza that promises to offer an occasion for benign, nostalgic reflection. One also recognizes the brilliant precision so common to Moore's poems.

Dürer would have seen a reason for living
    in a town like this, with eight stranded whales
to look at; with the sweet sea air coming into your house

on a fine day, from water etched
    with waves as formal as the scales
on a fish.   (CP, 5)

But the picture-perfect day on which "You can see a twenty-five- /
pound lobster; and fish nets arranged / to dry" turns out to be not very
peaceful at all. The seagulls, which "One by one in two's and three's . . .
keep / flying back and forth over the town clock," are buffeted by
the wind's turbulence as a storm "bends the salt / marsh grass, disturbs
stars in the sky and the / star on the steeple." Nothing in the poem
stands still or can be determined. One cannot be certain of the time of
day or the perspective of the viewer. Nor is it clear why the poem's "college student / named Ambrose sits on the hillside / with his not-native
books and hat / and sees boats // at sea progress white and rigid as if
in / a groove." Under this town's picturesque facade lurks deception
and imminent danger. Ambrose "knows by heart the antique sugar-
bowl shaped summerhouse of // interlacing slats." He also knows "the
pitch / of the church // spire, not true" (6–7).

When Moore presents the similarly contradictory—and in this case
precarious—experience of the poem's steeplejack, she uses her tightly
controlled form to show that the danger is both unexpected and absolute. In the tranquil setting

        a man in scarlet lets
    down a rope as a spider spins a thread;
    he might be part of a novel, but on the sidewalk a
    sign says C. J. Poole, Steeple-Jack,
        in black and white; and one in red
    and white says

Danger.   (6–7)

The church, Moore goes on to explain, "would be a fit haven" for an
unlikely group—"waifs, children, animals, prisoners, / and presidents
who have repaid / sin-driven // senators by not thinking about them." In
the final stanza, with the understatement that so frequently eludes those
readers who remain influenced by the myth of Marianne Moore, she ex-
plodes the false serenity that the poem has so carefully nurtured.

    It could not be dangerous to be living
        in a town like this, of simple people,
    who have a steeple-jack placing danger signs by the church
    while he is gilding the solid-

> pointed star, which on a steeple
> stands for hope.   (7)

In the same way that earlier a fine day did not exclude the "whirlwind
fife and drum of the storm," contradiction here reigns supreme. The star
on the steeple is merely gilded. It is solid not at its center but at its points.
It stands for hope, but only when on a steeple, in this case one which is
untrue. Moore tears down our easy assurance as effectively and methodically as she has constructed it, and the poem ends by making us
wonder whether, after all, Dürer really would have seen any reason for
living in such a deceptively serene place. "The Steeple-Jack" reveals a
Marianne Moore fascinated by brilliant precision but drawn as well to a
subsurface boiling with contradiction and hidden danger. New Criticism
called such contrasts balanced tensions. The precision of art was a welcome if temporary respite from the unpredictability and instability of
human actions. Such is not the case with Marianne Moore. Chaos triumphs in "The Steeple-Jack," and craftsmanship is just as unstable as
weather patterns and politicians. Nevertheless, the poem escapes defeat,
fear, and even pessimism. Fascination with danger leads to appreciation
of it.

Moore's acknowledgment that art cannot triumph over chaos leads
as well to her determination to accept human limitation. Her response
to the adversity of ordinary human limitations is most clear in "The
Pangolin," which is ironically Moore's best-known poem about armoring. Moving without either warning or transition from one subject (the
pangolin's armor) to another (human behavior), Moore constructs an
apology for human frailty and then a celebration of her accommodation
to that frailty. Privacy is the secret of equilibrium, and the pangolin is the
very embodiment of privacy. The spruce-cone regularity of its decorative
yet serviceable armor makes it a "night miniature artist engineer." The
pangolin, however, rejects and deflects any public recognition. Industrious and accomplished, the pangolin continues to choose that "we sel-
dom hear" of him. The poem endorses this choice, turns to human endeavor, and illustrates the versatility of such privacy in the human quest
to become "writing master to this world."

Moore begins the poem ironically by admitting that, once again, she
has chosen two of her favorite subjects—animals and armoring. But she
goes on to show that the pangolin's ingenious armor is as necessary as it
is unusual and decorative. Armor sometimes "seems extra," but for this
animal

> the closing ear-ridge—
>   or bare ear lacking this small
>   eminence and similarly safe

contracting nose and eye apertures
    impenetrably closable, are not   (117)

The armor aids the pangolin in his "exhausting solitary trips through
unfamiliar ground at night." On those journeys, he conserves energy
and protects himself by "stepping in the moonlight, / on the moonlight
peculiarly, that the outside / edges of his hands may bear the weight and
save the claws // for digging." Each example of the pangolin's behavior
emphasizes efficiency and equanimity. "Serpentined about the tree" in
what might ordinarily predict an intention to attack, the pangolin wisely

> draws
> away from danger unpugnaciously,
> with no sound but a harmless hiss; keeping

the fragile grace of the Thomas-
    of-Leighton Buzzard Westminster Abbey wrought-iron vine, or
rolls himself into a ball that has
    power to defy all effort to unroll it   (117)

Moore describes this posture as "strongly entailed" and shows that it
works quietly but effectively. The pangolin's stingproof scales resist outside pressures, so that he can form his own nestlike retreat "of rocks
closed with earth from inside, which he can thus darken." When under
attack, this "'Fearful, yet to be feared'" animal engulfs what he can, re-
gains his composure, and "will / then walk away / unhurt." Nevertheless, this thoroughly competent fighter prefers avoiding confrontation;
and his ingenuity in doing so completes Moore's demonstration of his
resourcefulness. "If unintruded on," the pangolin "cautiously works
down the tree, helped // by his tail," that "graceful tool, as prop or hand
or broom or ax, tipped like / an elephant's trunk with special skin."
    In contrast to the infallible instinct of this animal, Moore presents the
"simpletons [who] thought [the pangolin] a living fable / whom the
stones had nourished whereas ants had done / so." The folly of those
human simpletons then provides the starting point for Moore's defense
of "the being we call human." She poses an involved question, which
she follows with an "answer" that seems to answer nothing at all.

> If that which is at all were not forever,
> why would those who graced the spires
>   with animals and gathered there to rest, on cold luxurious
>   low stone seats—a monk and monk and monk—between the thus
>   ingenious roof-supports, have slaved to confuse
>   grace with kindly manner, time in which to pay a debt,

the cure for sins, a graceful use
   of what are yet
      approved stone mullions branching out across
      the perpendiculars? A sailboat

was the first machine.   (118–119)

The cryptic "answer" shows that man, maker of monuments and inventor of sailboats, combines love of beauty with judicious reasoning and with instinctive resourcefulness. "Slaving to make his life more sweet," he knows, like the pangolin, that he must "choose wisely how to use his strength." He makes monuments that are beautiful and that are also places of worship. Thus, in his own search for food, shelter, and security, this human animal becomes

a paper-maker like the wasp; a tractor of foodstuffs,
   like the ant; spidering a length
   of web from bluffs
      above a stream; in fighting, mechanicked
      like the pangolin   (119)

Nevertheless, those adaptive skills cannot protect man from human emotions, which leave him "capsizing in // disheartenment." Nor can they negate his uncomfortable recognition of the similarity in his fellow human beings—"'like does not like like that is obnoxious.'"

Ultimately, this vulnerable human animal triumphs by employing to his own advantage the intellect that had earlier led to his disheartenment. "Bedizened or stark / naked, man, the self, the being we call human," becomes "writing master to this world." He alone can do so because "Among animals, *one* has a sense of humor." It is an attribute that conveys "everlasting vigor" and "saves a few steps." Thus, although this human animal's special qualities do not save him from being "Unignorant, / modest and unemotional, and all emotion," he not only endures but rejoices. He enjoys the struggle and views it with pleasure rather than dismay. Moore's last stanza, the only self-contained one in her elaborately patterned poem, reveals this.

Not afraid of anything is he,
   and then goes cowering forth, tread paced to meet an obstacle
at every step. Consistent with the
      formula—warm blood, no gills, two pairs of hands and a few
      hairs—that
   is a mammal; there he sits in his own habitat,
      serge-clad, strong shod. The prey of fear, he, always

curtailed, extinguished, thwarted by the dusk, work partly
　　done,
says to the alternating blaze,
　　"Again the sun!
　　anew each day; and new and new and new,
　　that comes into and steadies my soul."　　　　　　　　(120)

Armed in conventional clothing, this prey of fear, this intelligent animal treads forth to meet each obstacle. The emotional triumph of that
human victory stands in marked contrast to the more stable but much
less rewarding "not unchain-like machine-like form and frictionless
creep" of the pangolin's daily endeavor. The poem celebrates both the
struggle and the victory of this armored writing master.

Like most of Moore's poetry, "The Pangolin" refrains from directly au-
tobiographical statement. The "writing master" is a "he" rather than a
"she," and by way of identification we learn only that he is "serge-clad,
strong shod." Nevertheless, the methodical ambition, the fearless determination, and the cautious but boundless energy of this writing master
are the same qualities that appear in Moore's letters and notebooks. The
portrait that emerges stands in direct contrast to those which emphasize
Moore's eccentricity. The strict control of her enabling straightjacket remains, but beneath and because of it, Moore's poems explore deepest
feeling with unshakable determination.

The self-assurance and the deeply emotional character of the writing
master who profits from the disguise are anticipated in an earlier Moore
poem, "Melancthon," which is unfortunately absent from Moore's woe-
fully abbreviated *Complete Poems*. The speaker's deliberate pace suggests
wisdom gained from years of experience. Elephant time does not acknowledge weightless, thoughtless self-absorption. Moore's speaker, an
elephant, is Black Earth (the title of the poem at one point), "black glass
through which no light // can filter" and an impenetrable "soul which
shall never // be cut into / by a wooden spear." [24] But the speaker is also
Melancthon (Philip), Martin Luther's colleague, who longed to be liberated from the wrath of dogmatic theologians and who tempered the Ref-
ormation with humanism. The poem goes on to develop this combination of privacy and openness. "Melancthon" addresses quite specifically
the difficulty and yet the obvious necessity of acknowledging another's
perspective while remaining oneself.

　　　　I see
　and I hear, unlike the
　　wandlike body of which one hears so much, which was made
　　to see and not to see; to hear and not to hear;

that tree-trunk without
roots, accustomed to shout
   its own thoughts to itself like a shell, maintained intact
   by who knows what strange pressure of the atmosphere; that

spiritual
brother to the coral-
   plant, absorbed into which, the equable sapphire light
   becomes a nebulous green. The I of each is to

the I of each
a kind of fretful speech
   which sets a limit on itself; the elephant is
   black earth preceded by a tendril?   (Col P, 47)

In contrast to fretful speech of rootless nomads, the elephant is stability
tempered by a desire to explore. This elephant, on whom "darts cannot
strike decisively the first // time" and whose skin is "cut / into checkers
by rut / upon rut of unpreventable experience," reaches out for new information. He can be receptive as well as self-sufficient. The poem's
opening lines announce this unmistakably. The speaker, mired in a bog
of his own making, clearly enjoys that murky setting.

Openly, yes.
with the naturalness
   of the hippopotamus or the alligator
   when it climbs out on the bank to experience the

sun, I do these
things which I do, which please
   no one but myself. Now I breathe and now I am submerged; but blemishes stand up and shout when the object

in view was a
renaissance; shall I say
   the contrary?   (Col P, 45)

The elephant sketches out the puzzle of his image and of his existence.
Like the hippopotamus or alligator, the elephant enjoys both mud baths
and sunbathing. In what seems like deliberate perversity, he enjoys sun-
ning himself all the more because of the mud coating that protects his
thick skin. In this protective covering, wrinkles, mud, and skin become
indistinguishable and therefore equally necessary—"Do away / with
[the covering] and I am myself done away with." The contented rise and
fall of the elephant's breath justify his claim that blemishes as well as per-

fection, emersion as well as submersion, will be part of any renaissance. Similarly, disguises are more than merely practical coverings and must be studied and explored rather than categorized and dismissed. The poem closes with a rhetorical question challenging those who would simply dismiss enigma to adopt a more open-minded point of view.

> Will
> depth be depth, thick skin be thick, to one who can see no
> beautiful element of unreason under it?   (Col P, 48)

Moore repeatedly champions this "beautiful element of unreason" even more so when she recognizes the discomfort such uncertainty sometimes produces. This is the discomfort she ridiculed in those Greeks who favored "smoothness, distrusting what was back / of what could not be clearly seen" and who insisted on "resolving with benevolent conclusiveness, 'complexities which still will be complexities as long as the world lasts.'"

In order to capture but not tame those complexities, Moore argues elsewhere for multiple perspective, unresolvable contradiction, and that "savage's romance," "accessibility to experience." This is especially true in "Marriage" and "An Octopus," which, taken as a contrasting pair of poems, illuminate some of Moore's personal complexity. In each of these poems, Moore's perspective is so inclusive and her point of view so likely to shift or detour at a moment's notice that it is almost impossible not to become lost in the Byzantine confusion that she presents with absolute precision. The two poems are also longer and more deeply emotional than most of Moore's other poems. In "Marriage," an all-seeing speaker catalogues pain and confusion. The poem ends pessimistically by equating artificially regulated promises with closed books and empty gestures. "An Octopus" records another sort of confusion. Rather than denying the fear involved in facing the unknown, the poem argues that the fear itself can become a positive adventure.

"Marriage" begins by categorizing its subject with unremitting equanimity and precision. The poem's subject, identified in its title, will be dismissed as

> This institution,
> perhaps one should say enterprise
> out of respect for which
> one says one need not change one's mind
> about a thing one has believed in,
> requiring public promises
> of one's intention
> to fulfill a private obligation   (CP, 62)

Moore continues the attack by piling one devastating anecdote upon another. Marriage is both preposterous and painful. As in "Melancthon," Moore ridicules insincere attempts at communication. Here, however, the mistaken approach leads to warfare. Instead of conversing, the participants in that war exchange mechanical nonsequiturs.

"*I* should like to be alone";
to which the visitor replies,
"I should like to be alone;
why not be alone together?"   (62–63)

Beneath this "conversation" lurks a subsurface of churning passion that recognizes beauty but distorts the perception.

Below the incandescent stars
below the incandescent fruit,
the strange experience of beauty;
its existence is too much;
it tears one to pieces
and each fresh wave of consciousness
is poison.   (63)

Indeed, overwhelming passion so distorts perception that even pristine beauty leads to disaster. Such is the case in the lines describing the poem's occasionally nameless "he," who in this case becomes Adam.

he has beauty also;
it's distressing—the O thou
to whom from whom,
without whom nothing—Adam;
"something feline,
something colubrine"—how true!
a crouching mythological monster
in that Persian miniature of emerald mines,
raw silk—ivory white, snow white,
oyster white and six others—
that paddock full of leopards and giraffes—
long lemon-yellow bodies
sown with trapezoids of blue.
Alive with words,
vibrating like a cymbal
touched before it has been struck,
he has prophesied correctly—

the industrious waterfall,
"the speedy stream
which violently bears all before it,
at one time silent as the air
and now as powerful as the wind."   (63–64)

This same vibrant Adam, "Treading chasms / on the uncertain footing of a spear," finally becomes so self-absorbed that his "formal customary strain" of speech and thought allows no intrusion of undesirable fact. Beauty disintegrates and turns sour as Adam inevitably

perceives what it was not
intended that he should;
"he experiences a solemn joy
in seeing that he has become an idol."   (64)

"She" is no less attractive and no less able to resist her own charm. In each case, the excess arises from a common error.

The fact forgot
that "some have merely rights
while some have obligations,"
he loves himself so much,
he can permit himself
no rival in that love.
She loves herself so much,
she cannot see herself enough—
a statuette of ivory on ivory,
the logical last touch
to an expansive splendor
earned as wages for work done:
one is not rich but poor
when one can always seem so right.   (68)

Wrong from the start, then, any attempt at marriage, "this amalgamation which can never be more / than an interesting impossibility," will be doomed to failure. Moore's criticism has been impartially distributed since each participant in the union shares the same faults. Her attack becomes even more successful because she reinforces this impartiality with relentless dispassion. The poem offers neither a death blow nor an alternative to the institution but a depressing version of half success. The partners are sentenced to "cycloid inclusiveness," a "striking grasp of opposites / opposed each to the other, not to unity. . . ." Moore's argument that there can be no respite in this struggle intensifies throughout the poem until she asks a question to which she already knows the answer.

> What can one do for them—
> these savages
> condemned to disaffect
> all those who are not visionaries
> alert to undertake the silly task
> of making people noble?   (68)

Since nothing can be done to aid the self-deluded, Moore ruthlessly concludes that this naive but mistaken belief in the efficacy of "public promises . . . to fulfill a private obligation" dictates that "the statesmanship / of an archaic Daniel Webster / persists to their simplicity of temper / as the essence of the matter." Meaningless contradiction, a passive symbol of church or state, and the withdrawal of personal contact close the poem and become Moore's enigmatic representation of "the essence of the matter."

> 'Liberty and union
> now and forever';
>
> the Book on the writing-table;
> the hand in the breast-pocket,"   (70)

One can claim to be attempting liberty and union, but the combination is a farce. A book on a writing table may block as many thoughts as it inspires, and if the capitalization in "Book" signifies the Bible, a book Marianne Moore certainly knew well, the passive image is even more damaging. A hand in the breast pocket cannot offer to shake another nor can it signal any other traditional pledge of disarmament. The posture is unequivocally closed and defensive. The institution has been dismissed. The issue is closed.

"Marriage" is an unusual poem in the Moore canon because its treatment is more openly personal than that of most of her poems. More important, Moore's treatment of passion, confusion, and deluded vision is undeniably negative. The fact that her sensuous language vividly captures the attraction of one party to another only intensifies the shock of the rest of the poem. In most poems, Moore treats such confusion and deluded vision as positive qualities, as opportunities for wordplay or enjoyment.

Thus, as if to counter the dismal effect of "Marriage," Moore follows the shock of her conclusion with another long, dense poem, "An Octopus," which begins somewhat ominously and quickly turns that mood into joyful appreciation of the indecipherable density of Mount Tacoma's glacier. Every specimen of disarray offers a form of delight, precisely because of its inherent and unfathomable contradiction. A visitor to the glacier finds that its density of growth makes vision difficult, even misleading; but he enjoys the opacity, which he finds

> under the polite needles of the larches
> "hung to filter, not to intercept the sunlight"—
> met by tightly wattled spruce-twigs
> "conformed to an edge like clipped cypress
> as if no branch could penetrate the cold beyond its company"
>
> (CP, 71)

It is thus contrarily pleasant to discover that "Completing a circle, / you have been deceived into thinking that you have progressed." The confusion "prejudices you in favor of itself." Throughout the poem, Moore holds in suspension and demonstrates the simultaneous presence of the two opposing qualities of the glacier. Although "damned for its sacrosanct remoteness," it attracts those who damn that remoteness while engaged in attempts to "'conquer the main peak of Mount Tacoma.'" Nevertheless, combined with that remoteness, "Relentless accuracy is the nature of this octopus / with its capacity for fact." Offering partial shelter, the mountain "receives one under winds that 'tear the snow to bits / and hurl it like a sandblast / shearing off twigs and loose bark from the trees.'" It also challenges its visitors' perceptions, producing questions such as this one.

> Is "tree" the word for these things
> "flat on the ground like vines"?
> some "bent in a half circle with branches on one side
> suggesting dust-brushes, not trees;
> some finding strength in union, forming little stunted groves
> their flattened mats of branches shrunk in trying to escape"
> from the hard mountain "planed by ice and polished by the wind"—
>
> (CP, 76)

The poem ends with an explosion of motion that finds mysterious calm and self-possession on the mountain, even in the midst of unpredictable violence. The "symmetrically-pointed" octopus survives the violence of an avalanche because of its "curtain of powdered snow launched like a waterfall." Moore wants us, in the words of another poem of impossible opposites, to "believe it / despite reason to think not" (CP, 160).

"The Octopus" thus reverses the mood of "Marriage" without changing its basic ingredients—equilibrium in the midst of chaos. In "Marriage" the speaker stands outside the chaos, horrified at the inexorable self-destruction of the poem's protagonists. In "The Octopus" the chaos is even more bewildering, but survival and even genuine enjoyment result from complete and unquestioning immersion in the chaos. Moore's later poems continue this trend. She presents every possible form of contradiction, chaos, or confusion with such absolute precision that the poems seem to be flirting with nonsense.

"Then the Ermine," which urges belief despite unreason, defends this method by appealing to one of Moore's perennial favorites, Dürer. One need not shout one's accomplishments in order to achieve spectacular effects. In fact, part of the pleasure comes from unexpected surprises when one perceives deliberately hidden effects. The challenge of accurate perception thus falls to the reader.

> Foiled explosiveness is yet
> a kind of prophet,
>
> a perfecter, and so a concealer—
>   with the power of implosion;
> like violets by Dürer,
> even darker.   (CP, 161)

The genius of Dürer's work, in Moore's estimation, is that it is a calculated distortion of the details he purported to portray quite accurately. Moore's own accurate distortions, particularly as they turn toward implosion, so dominate her late work that the poems become almost impenetrable. When they turn to epigram, as they often do, the foil works so effectively and the clipped endings seem so artificial that the poems risk being dismissed as embarrassing, lamely occasional works, devoid of power. A closer look reveals that Moore's late poems, while still treating her early subjects, such as armoring, complexity, and the difficulty of accurate perception, continue with increasing force to undermine every expectation of what poetry is and can do. This power is Moore's subject in "Baseball and Writing / Suggested by post-game broadcasts," which clearly plays with quotations, going beyond what she once described as "lines in which the chief interest is borrowed." Moore captures in a riotous but absolutely controlled volley of observations and partial quotations from innumerable viewpoints the rapidly shifting perceptions and moods of a baseball game and the fragmentary nature of broadcast coverage of games. In what might serve as an apologia for her difficult style, Moore opens the poem by anticipating and then answering a question.

> Fanaticism? No. Writing is exciting
> and baseball is like writing.

> You can never tell with either
>   how it will go
>   or what you will do   (CP, 221)

This is certainly true for Moore as well. Her poetry, at times intricately patterned and at other times expansive and sprawling, contains precise, half-hidden, internal, and off rhymes. Her subjects range from contemporary politics to scientific discovery, and the "notes" she provided to document her "hybrid method of composition" sometimes raise more questions than the poems themselves. Moore has consistently been praised for the craft of her poetry, but less frequently for the remarkable things she did with that craft. She used the relentless accuracy of her poetry to undermine what she disliked in the European and British tradition that American writers had inherited. Thus, instead of writing what in "England" she called outdated poetry, "all of museum quality," this writing master discarded the traditional music of the lyre and composed "fragmentary and convoluted" work suitable for an

> America where there
> is the little old ramshackle victoria in the south,
> where cigars are smoked on the street in the north;
> where there are no proof-readers, no silkworms, no digressions;
> the wild man's land; grassless, linksless, languageless country
>   in which letters are written
> not in Spanish, not in Greek, not in Latin, not in shorthand,
> but in plain American which cats and dogs can read!   (CP, 46)

The poetry isn't quite that simple, but it breaks as many rules, violates as many traditions, and reverses as many expectations as the America portrayed in these lines. The writing master who composed them was a curious woman, unfathomable even to her friends. The intensity of Moore's cynicism in "Marriage" is matched, curiously enough, only by her fascination with every other sort of confusion and contradiction. The pattern Moore imposed upon this confusion begins to emerge in her earliest prose essays, in their subject matter, and, even more important, in her method of composition.

2 ▪ Compact, Subtle Essays

THE PORTRAIT of Moore that emerged in the previous chapter from her own papers, from the comments of friends, and from some of her poems helps to expose and weaken the control of the myth that has been constructed around her; but it does not automatically make her poetry more accessible. Lacking transitions, sprinkled randomly with phrases enclosed for no discernible reason in quotation marks, neither traditionally patterned nor wholly without imposed form, the poems challenge, frustrate, and sometimes deliberately mislead readers. Moore occasionally referred to the "critical trend" of her poems, but the critical statements they make are often resolutely enigmatic. "No Swan So Fine" is perhaps the most outrageous example of this practice since it purports to be so accessible and orderly. The poem clearly makes a value judgment about stasis versus open-endedness in art, but it is not easy to determine what Moore's judgment is. Moore accentuates the problem by her clipped epigrammatic ending, which only seems to imply a definitive statement.

The practice is common in Moore's poetry, and it appears in her critical essays as well. Often as difficult and unyielding as the poems, the essays have frequently been called impressionistic. They have also been dismissed on the grounds that Moore's decorum kept her from printing unfavorable comments on any subject. It was, in fact, Moore's belief that one could condemn a book more effectively by ignoring it than by attacking it. The essays she did publish are thus rarely negative. They are also curious pieces of work, although "quaint" would be the word in terms of the myth of Moore's personal image. The essays seem most often to stray at will from one subject to another. Many of them also appear to suffer from excessive quotation, so much so that one can discern neither Moore's interpretation and evaluation nor her own prose style. These faults, however, are part of Moore's deliberate plan, one which reflects the inclusive thinking, the close attention to detail, and the liberal use of quotation found in her early letters and notebooks. Her compact, subtle essays work contrapuntally, often in imitative form, so that Moore's style and organization pay nearly silent tribute to her subjects. That near silence has misled some of Moore's readers. They find politesse or lack of conviction and miss her specific critical judgments as well as her theoretical statements on the art of reading and the act of criticism. In treating Moore's essays, this chapter will necessarily examine at length both her own prose and the quotations she weaves into her text. The essays are seamless wholes that belie their essential complexity. Once in Moore's possession, borrowed prose becomes inseparable and nearly indistinguishable from her own. Reading lengthy excerpts from Moore's essays will be the chief method of this chapter since such work is essential both to recognizing Moore's style and to grasping the outer calm and inner jumble that are their essence.

As a prelude to reading Moore's essays, some of her best-known poems provide helpful background. In particular, recognizing the fact that Moore's curious mixture of outer calm and inner jumble also exists in her poetry makes the task of breaking through the surface of her essays a bit easier. This mixture is especially evident in the cluster of poems that announce with considerable critical fanfare that they prefer jumbles to the perfection of finished works of art.

"Critics and Connoisseurs," "In the Days of Prismatic Colour," and "Picking and Choosing" express Moore's principles in capsule form. "No Swan So Fine" puts them into action. What we think of as art need not necessarily be finished, balanced, or polished. In "Critics and Connoisseurs," for example, the speaker rejects any prejudice toward the lure of artistic perfection and praises instead the "great amount of poetry in unconscious / fastidiousness." If criticism tries to communicate how what gives us pleasure manages to do so, the subject matter for such criticism is limitless.

> Certain Ming
>   products, imperial floor-coverings of coach-
> wheel yellow, are well enough in their own way but I have seen
>   something
>   that I like better—a
>   mere childish attempt to make an imperfectly bal-
>   lasted animal stand up,
>   similar determination to make a pup
>   eat his meat from the plate.   (CP, 38)

The boundary between "art" and "other" begins to disappear when perfect form ceases to be the definitive criterion.

Moore expands upon this idea in "In the Days of Prismatic Colour" by asserting that, in making judgments, "Truth is no Apollo / Belvedere, no formal thing." One must acknowledge complexity and allow it "to be

the pestilence that it is." Contrarily unwilling to apologize for such difficulty, Moore insists that reading and the inevitable evaluation that ac-
companies reading must be neither avoided nor underestimated.

> Literature is a phase of life. If one is afraid of it,
> the situation is irremediable; if one approaches it familiarly,
> what one says of it is worthless.   (CP, 45)

Hard work, but not necessarily specialized labor, will get the job done
since "done" needs to be redefined as well.

> only rudimentary behavior is necessary to put us on the scent.
> "A right good salvo of barks," a few strong wrinkles puckering
>   the skin between the ears, is all we ask.   (45)

Indeed, wrinkled foreheads rather than serene transcendence seem to be
the effect Moore was working for.

"No Swan So Fine" illustrates this apparently deliberate effect quite
well. Several years in the making, the poem grew out of two newspaper
clippings, one reporting on the sale of a pair of Louis XV candelabra and
another on the restoration of the gardens of the Palace of Versailles.
From the second, which appeared in the *New York Times Magazine*,
Moore copied Percy Philip's whimsical note that the statues on the Versailles grounds seemed to be protesting the dullness of their surroundings without the courts of the Kings Louis. To that clipping, Moore
added the caption from an accompanying photograph, which showed
the temporarily stilled fountains: "There is no water so still as the dead
fountain of Versailles."[1] Moore changed the quotation slightly and used
it to open the poem. But, without any guide to indicate the context of
the quotation and therefore its tone of voice, one cannot be certain
whether Moore's next sentence is meant to be naive, ironic, or regretful.

> "No water so still as the
>   dead fountains of Versailles." No swan,
> with swart blind look askance
> and gondoliering legs, so fine
>   as the chintz china one with fawn-
> brown eyes and toothed gold
> collar on to show whose bird it was.   (CP, 19)

Although the second sentence begins forthrightly enough, it quickly
confuses itself. The water of the fountain seems serene, even appealing,
and the real-life swan rather clumsy by contrast. But the "chintz china"
swan, which ought to be as appealing as the formal fountains, ends up
being trapped by the control and ownership that its "toothed gold col-

lar" represents. Moore's second stanza promises to rectify this ambivalence when it goes on to describe the elegance of the setting in which this lifeless swan resides. Once again, though, Moore undercuts this response as skillfully as she creates it.

> Lodged in the Louis Fifteenth
>   Candelabrum-tree of cockscomb-
> tinted buttons, dahlias,
> sea urchins, and everlastings,
>   it perches on the branching foam
> of polished sculptured
> flowers—at ease and tall. The king is dead.   (19)

What does "The king is dead" mean? And what does that reveal about the dead fountains and about why the real-life swan is not "so fine as" its artificial counterpart? On one level, the poem reads as an outraged indictment of artifice and stasis. In this case, the second sentence reads ironically and defends the real-life swan not in spite of but precisely because of his imperfections. The elegant setting of the china swan, amidst "polished sculptured flowers," becomes a prison. Its beauty lacks spirit, just as the king lacks life. In this scenario, the opening quotation reveals the anonymous observer's misguided nostalgia and romantic reverence for whatever has been controlled, stopped, and in this case deadened by artifice. Responding to that speaker's erroneous viewpoint, the rest of the poem reads as a defense of the candelabra's artifice. Admittedly, the waters of the fountains, like the king, are lifeless; but artifice guarantees continued recognition beyond any organic life cycle. It creates the elegance of the china swan perched with ironic detachment "—at ease and tall" in its excessively decorative and controlled surroundings. That same artifice continues to elicit awe, even when its beauty is reduced to static potential. Initially such artifice excludes the mundane imperfections and "the swart blind look askance" of passing moments. Ultimately, it outlasts its vulnerable creators. The poem thus argues effectively for each point of view.

The double nature of Moore's argument is unusual, especially in light of William Butler Yeats's treatment of a related type of ambivalance. Moore's "No Swan So Fine," published in 1932, five years after Yeats's "Sailing to Byzantium," captures the allure of that poem's "artifice of eternity," but does not capitulate to its temptations. When Yeats's speaker vows to escape from the place that "is no country for old men," he expects the retreat, whatever its limitations, to succeed.

> Once out of nature I shall never take
> My bodily form from any natural thing,

> But such a form as Grecian goldsmiths make
> Of hammered gold and gold enamelling
> To keep a drowsy Emperor awake;
> Or set upon a golden bough to sing
> To lords and ladies of Byzantium
> Of what is past, or passing, or to come.[2]

Never one to assure or coddle her readers in any way, Moore hints at the same lure of escape, deftly questions its efficacy, and then steps aside without offering any conclusion. She repeats that practice frequently, but the puzzle of no conclusion is the only common feature in the various poems in which she does so.

The two-sided message of "No Swan So Fine" thus serves as Moore's response to Yeats's thwarted dream in "Sailing to Byzantium." In the Yeats poem, the golden bird's escape is at best partial and imperfect. Even if in the "artifice of eternity" Yeats's singer achieves its desired form "Of hammered and gold enamelling," its song might serve as trivial a purpose as keeping a "drowsy Emperor awake." Or it might sing only "Of what is past, or passing, or to come." Unable to sing of real-world creatures, whether "Fish, flesh, or fowl," its song can be heard only by those "lords and ladies of Byzantium," removed as they are from the world of "Whatever is begotten, born and dies." Moore's answer is both a regression and a progression, just as she intends it to be. "No Swan So Fine" does not solve Yeats's dilemma. In fact, it refuses to long for one of Byzantium's alternatives. Moore sets up a dialectical opposition and refuses to resolve it. One longs for strict forms capable of containing and controlling the complexity of the age, but a form that hopes to control the chaos automatically becomes suspect.

Just as the strict form of "No Swan So Fine" stands in sharp contrast to its open-ended argument, Moore's critical essays carry a similar double message.[3] They seem to say that they are making no critical judgments; but in saying so, they make specific evaluations and set out critical principles for reading. The essays differ from one another in approach and subject matter and do not grow out of a predetermined point of view. Instead, they share an intense concern with the style of the work under review. This interest, as well as Moore's practice of embedding quotations from the work under review in her own essay, result in essays that resemble and, in fact, deliberately imitate the style of the work she is discussing. Both in the essays and in the poetry, Moore's imitative form enacts her content in her style.

When Hugh Kenner described Moore's poetry as a "heavy system of nouns . . . without the syntactic lubricants that slide us past a comparison,[4] he might well have been describing her essays. Highly compact, they join seemingly unrelated subjects as a means of working toward her peculiarly subtle critical points. Donald Hall called the essays "impressionistic and unaimed."[5] Bernard Engle decided that "Miss Moore's real career was in poetry" and condescendingly dismissed her prose as merely "graceful presentations of observations and impressions, the kind of statement one might expect from a good reader rather than from a professional critic."[6] Kenneth Burke, on the other hand, praises Moore's essays for their "precision" and their "technique." He explains that Moore's characteristic gift was her ability to praise in the very act of observing. When Moore's subject is another writer, her "generosity" becomes "an act of collaboration."[7] Burke's evaluation thus recognizes that both Moore's contrapuntal organization and her imitative form are integral parts of her criticism. Two very early Moore essays, "Samuel Butler" and "The Accented Syllable," illustrate the indirection that would continue to characterize her later work. The brevity of the first essay permits quoting it in its entirety.

SAMUEL BUTLER

Butler is a blackthorn stick in the hands of the optimist. "Surely we may do whatever we like, and the better we like it, the better we shall do it," illustrates his idea of the values of literary boundaries and prohibitions. To set the matter forth uncurtailed. "It has been said, 'thou shalt not masquerade in costumes not of thine own period.' But the history of art is the history of revivals. Surely we may do whatever we like and the better we like it, the better we shall do it. The great thing is to make sure that we like the style we choose better than we like any other; that we engraft on it whatever we hear that we think will be a good addition and depart from it wherever we dislike it. If a man does this, he may write in the style of the year one, and not be an anachronism."

The fact of Butler's unwillingness to assume the official character of "scrutineer" has not impaired his serviceability. One does not love a man the less for his unwillingness to say, "I have examined the credentials of other people; I have plucked masks from hypocrites' faces; I have stood nearby to see that no undeserving person got a crumb." What does impair his serviceability is a disability shared by him in common with most slaves—the inability to enjoy the progress which he was able to promote.[8]

Here is the characteristic politeness and the "distracting surface brilliance" that Hugh Kenner (*Homemade World*, 111) found in many of Moore's poems and that resulted largely from her inclusion of quotations within her own work. There is more in the essay as well. Moore begins with what might seem a simple statement, but the specificity of her language is conscious and effective. The blackthorn stick is in the hand and not the side of the optimist. It can be used both as a weapon against those nonoptimists who would set stringent literary boundaries and also as a support in pursuing new literary styles. The serviceability of the blackthorn stick is not at all impaired by Butler's unwillingness to scrutinize or to pass judgment, but by his disability or inability to enjoy the progress—a freedom to create one's own style—which he himself promotes. Moore's cryptic comment here is difficult to discern, but her alteration of "disability" into "inability" is more than an elegant variation on her use of "serviceability." Since *inability* connotes inner shortcomings rather than the outer impairments that *disability* suggests, Moore manages with typical understatement to criticize Butler's failure to *enjoy* what he himself was promoting. The essay is important because it shows that as early as her first published essay Moore was arguing against stringent literary boundaries and promoting enjoyment as an acceptable criterion for evaluating artists or their work.

This viewpoint is essential to understanding Moore's intriguing and problematic essay, "The Accented Syllable." Even more helpful is the discovery among Moore's manuscripts of an unpublished portion of the essay.[9] In its published form, "The Accented Syllable" seems unfocused and self-contradictory. With the unpublished section restored, however, one quickly sees that Moore's argument is deliberately dialectical and that in it she anticipates, at the height of imagism, postmodern American poetry's concern for capturing tone of voice. She manages, at the same time, to anticipate contemporary critical method by enacting the content of her essay in her style.

"The Accented Syllable" begins abruptly by asserting, "For the most part in what we read, it is the meaning rather than the tone of voice which gives us pleasure."[10] It is, then, unsettling to discover that in the rest of the essay Moore argues cogently—but inexplicably, considering her opening—for the importance of an author's tone of voice. Defining tone of voice as "that intonation in which the accents which are responsible for it are so unequivocal as to persist no matter under what circumstances the syllables are read or by whom they are read," Moore claims that by it an author either compels or repels us. She then guides us through a remarkably complex set of assertions and examples designed to prove her point. Moore claims that Poe's voice, flavored with artifice, whether he writes history or fiction, is successful in the tales since it intensifies the artificiality of his drawing-room conversations. But, Moore argues, Poe's essays on the literati of New York are not sound because he lacks imagination. Here Poe's tone works against him, becoming a "straining for rarity and an unmistakable tone of condescension." It is also true, Moore continues, that "written tones of voice may resemble each other and that a distinctive tone of voice employed by one author may resemble that same tone of voice employed by another." In supporting this assertion Moore creates another problem. She claims that the examples she has chosen from Poe are "as like Butler's notes as any of Butler's notes are like each other." But without any examples from Butler, it is difficult to concede Moore that point. Moore seems unaware of this gap in her argument and goes on to insist that "the fact that a tone of voice is not invariably a distinctly personal one does not alter the fact that the tone of voice does contribute to or detract from the aesthetic effect of a piece of writing." Her argument in support of this assertion is as brief as it is amusing.

So far as free verse is concerned, it is the easiest thing in the world to create one intonation in the image of another until finally one has assembled a bouquet of vocal exclamation points. I can read the following advertisement with a great deal of pleasure but I am not sure that it would give me pleasure to read this indentical advertisement every day in the week. An intonation must have meaning behind it to support it, or it is not worth much:

> Venus pencils are made in seventeen black and two copying degrees, each degree guaranteed never to vary: softest and blackest, very very soft and very black, very soft and very black, very soft and black, soft and black, soft, soft medium, firm, medium hard, hard, very hard, extra hard, very very hard and firm, extra extra hard and firm, extra extra hard and extra firm, hardest and firmest.

Moore's first sentence here is cogent and remarkably prophetic in its criticism of imagism carried to the extreme, but her argument is not altogether convincing. The Venus pencil advertisement, curious enough for an exhibit in a critical argument, undoubtedly has accents "so unequivocal as to persist," but it also has meaning. These are not nonsense words; and to Moore, a talented sketcher herself, the words must have had very specific meaning. What Marianne Moore claims is that it might not *continue* to give her pleasure and thus "is not worth much." But it is difficult to accept this evaluation and even more difficult to justify Moore's abrupt return to her opening remark.

The discovery of the excised section of the essay settles these problems. In the manuscript, Moore's second sentence is this: "In the case of the following groups of words, however, I am inclined to think that the meaning has very little to do with the pleasure the words give us." There follow these twelve quotations:

> "Then Louisa went into the kitchen and cried for it is exasperating to be unjustly accused." Strindberg: EASTER AND OTHER PLAYS

"And verse? Why I even composed a whole drama in imitation of Manfred. Among the characters was a ghost with blood on its breast, and not his own blood observe, but the blood of all humanity." Turgenef: RUDIN

"Tom when very young, had presented Sophia with a little bird which he had taken from the nest, had nursed up and taught to sing." TOM JONES

"One would hate to have to live in the world which Mr. X describes but one is delightfully conscious of the fact that one will never have to." J. B. Kerfoot: LIFE

"As I have said over and over again, if I think something that I know and greatly like" (in music) "no matter whose it is, is appropriate, I appropriate it." Butler: Note 122

"A cognate essay is *On Description in Poetry* by Mr. A Clutton-Brock, who contends, firstly, that beauty in poetic description is *irrelevant* unless it adds to the cumulative powers of the whole, and secondly, that it must be judged not by absolute standards but by its relation *to the theme.* Sound notions, these. The first might be taken to heart by certain modern bards; the second, by their critics." Books of the Month: ENGLISH REVIEW, January, 1912

"It is true enough to say that everybody is selfish provided we add, and unselfish." Cabot: WHAT MEN LIVE BY

"Does Mr. Shaw admit that he has blundered? Not a bit of it. He assures the spectators that while in one sense the theme is not the 'opening theme' because it does not open the work, in a higher, subtler sense it is the opening theme inasmuch as the music passes into it by 'an irresistible gravitation.' Mr. Shaw's week, I suppose, begins with Tuesday afternoon." "The Arts and Crafts of Bernard Shaw." Reprinted in the TRANSCRIPT, Boston, September 16, 1914.

"Of course I knew all that down in the cellars of my being, but upstairs all the same I had the sense of guilt and expiation, this anxious doubt that perhaps all that great, gloomy, mediaeval business of saints and nuns and bones and relics and miracles and icons and calvaries and cells and celibacy and horsehair shirts and blood and dirt and tears, was true ofter all!" Zangwill: DREAMERS OF THE GHETTO.

"Androcles is probably Mr. Shaw himself and right glad we are to see him." ENGLISH REVIEW, October, 1913.

"Impartial? Never." LIFE

and the English to the footnote to one of Augier's plays: "Three chops well peppered."

Each of these quotations captures a distinctive tone of voice and thereby provides pleasure. The Butler passage, from his then recently published *Notebooks*, also supplies the necessary comparison with Poe's critical prose and suggests a criterion that Marianne Moore employed in her own writing: ". . . if I think something that I know and greatly like . . . no matter whose it is, is appropriate, I appropriate it." Moore appropriated these quotations and the Venus pencil advertisement because they enabled her to argue dialectically for the simultaneous importance of meaning and tone of voice. Furthermore, in arguing for the importance of capturing tone of voice, Moore isolated the shortcomings of imagism and anticipated postmodern poetic concerns, particularly those of William Carlos Williams and Charles Olson, who sought to capture in poems and on paper what Moore called "that intonation in which the accents which are responsible for it are so unequivocal as to persist no matter under what circumstances the syllables are read or by whom they are read." Finally, and here the discovery of the unpublished section of the essay is most important, Moore assembled her own bouquet of vocal exclamation points and thus begins the process of enacting the content of an essay in its form.

Another early piece, Moore's "Note on T. S. Eliot's Book," begins with a complaint in order to argue that evaluation must begin not from predetermined criteria but from an attempt to discover principles within the work under consideration. Claiming to be offended by Eliot's "Portrait of a Lady," Moore simply but humorously remarked, "It might be advisable for Mr. Eliot to publish a fangless edition of *Prufrock and Other Observations* for the gentle reader who likes his literature, like breakfast coffee or grapefruit, sweetened." Moore goes on to suggest that by rearranging the poems Eliot might soften the blow of "the ungallantry, the youthful cruelty of the substance of "Portrait." [11] By calling the review merely "A Note on T. S. Eliot's Book," Moore leads her reader to expect informal comment. Her subsequent change of topic thus seems whimsical until one realizes that Moore's lack of transition is part of the contrapuntal arrangement of her dialectical argument.

Whistler in his post-impressionistic English studies—and these poems are not entirely unlike Whistler's studies—had the advantage of his more static medium, of a somewhat more romantic temperament, and of the fact that the objects he painted half-hid their ugliness under shadows and the haze of distance. But Eliot deals with life, with beings and things who live and move almost nakedly before his individual mind's eye—in the darkness, in the early sunlight, and in the fog. Whatever one may feel about sweetness in literature, there is the word honesty, and this man is a faithful friend of the objects he portrays; altogether unlike the sentimentalist who really stabs them treacherously in the back while pretending affection.   (37)

Moore's point here is that while one may be offended by the brutality of the images in *Prufrock,* Eliot's vivid presentation, softened neither by the half-hidden ugliness and romantic temperament of Whistler nor by the half truths of a sentimentalist, becomes the value of his poems. She admits that this may not be enjoyable and therefore defends Eliot's ability to deal with life, "with beings and things who live and move" (37). The poem *is* offensive; the poem *is* good. The contradiction will not be resolved, and the point of view that sets out the dialectic becomes crucial in Moore's editorship of *The Dial* and continues to appear in her poetry.

These three essays represent Moore's early use of lengthy quotation and the initial stages of her imitative form. The first essay to develop these methods fully appeared in *The Dial* and takes a nonverbal text as its subject. "Is the Real Actual?" progresses in serpentine fashion toward Moore's evaluation and recreation of the sculpture of Alfeo Faggi. In part, just because the essay takes a nonverbal text as its subject, it becomes a striking example of Moore's ability to enact content in form. Moore begins the essay by conveying a sense of the effects Faggi achieved in several pieces of sculpture. She recalls the "smooth dark surface of the Tagore like a ripe olive, the bone-white, weathered aspect of the [Robert] Frost, the misty waxlike bloom of the Eve as on bayberries or iris stalks, and the tarnish and glint of fire in Faggi's *Dante.*"[12] Moore's description of the Dante piece becomes the central exhibit of the review. Remarking that it is perhaps impossible to grasp the nature of the phenomenon that Dante represents, Moore praises Faggi's bronze piece for its apparent synthesis of the biographical conjecture and historical certainties of Dante's life. She then recreates the sculpture in prose:

In this robustly compact bronze like some colossal gold ingot stood erect, obviously intended to represent a man but not brutishly male, with the look of the athlete made lean, with the action in repose of the spiritual potentate, one sees the man as one has imagined him, the student of "philosophy, theology, astrology, arthmetic, and geometry, turning over many curious books, watching and sweating in his studies," with a view of the world founded as Croce says, on faith, judgment and bound by a stong will, commanding like a wall of solid water, the incredulity of minds egotistical and as shallow as a fish-wafer—too idle to think. In the intellectuality, the distilled impersonal spiritual force of Mr. Faggi's Dante, one recalls Giotto's superiority to interest in masculinity or femininity *per se;* the inadvertent muscularity and angelic grace of his male figures—the faces of his madonnas and female saints, like the faces of stalwart boys. In the shoulders compact like a bulldog's, in the nostrils built for expansion in action under physical stress sunk under long imposed restraint, the horizontal eyebrows, raised cheekbones of the ascetic, the iron skull, the substantial character of the face as of an iron crow, the mobile expression of the mouth—not incompatible with the gaiety of which Croce and other authorities are convinced—the cap like war, set from the face as if to indicate hope; the collar, round like an ecclesiastic's; the wakeful reserve of the lowered eyes—we have "the ardor, admiration and fury" of the politician, the distilled supersensory sentience of the seer—the man who was "the product of a nation of scholars and doctors who were artists." In the animating force of this bronze in its setting of physical power, is embodied the spiritual axiom that Dante has come to be.   (622)

This passage captures the power Moore sensed in the piece and also illustrates the synthetic and allusive method of Moore's essays. The title of this essay—"Is the Real Actual?"—forewarns that the Faggi exhibit is not the only subject of the essay. Instead, it is simultaneously about Faggi, Dante, and spirituality. By supplying the connectives that Moore deliberately left out of the essay, one can reconstruct her allusive, creative process and enjoy the exhibits that she has assembled.

Moore begins the essay by indicating the direction of her interest. "The preoccupation to-day is with the actual. The work of Alfeo Faggi, exhibited last year and with important additions this year at the Bourgeois Gallery, is especially for the thinker, presenting as it does solidly and in variety, a complete contrast to the fifty-fathom deep materialism of the hour" (620). Moore then presents the following sinuous argument. Spiritual imagination is what enables an artist to interpret subjects that are spiritual—that is, those which derive feeling from the subject rather than bring feeling to it. This spiritual quality is present in Faggi's sculpture, particularly the Ka and the Dante, but also in his depictions of Robert Jones, Isamu Noguchi, and Eve. Even Faggi's choice of medium in each piece of work reflects his sensitive interpretation of the subject. And along with the great range of his subjects and medium, there is also a creative unity in the lines and shapes of his work. But even for an artist with considerable technical skills, the task of portraying spiritual subjects is a difficult one. "Face to face with such sincere expressions, one suspects that in the vulgarity and peremptoriness of one's passion, either in praise or in blame, one may find himself as St. Augustine says he was prior to his conversion, 'like a dog snapping at flies'"   (621).

Moore then returns to her opening idea, stating that Faggi's sculpture shows that the realm of the spiritual is the only one in which the real (the very essence of a thing) can also be made actual. Finally, Moore contradicts Arthur Symons's contention that we cannot comprehend a nature more spiritual than our own and that this shortcoming was the reason for Boccaccio's failure to capture Dante on canvas. On the contrary, Moore insists, Faggi did capture the real in the actual—the essence of unfathomable spirituality in bronze. "Those who have studied biographical conjecture and the historical certainties of Dante's life will be grateful to Mr. Faggi for his synthesis of what is the feeling or at least the apprehension of so many" (622). This is the argument that led up to Moore's recreation of the Dante, her synthesis of the reading she herself had done on Dante, and the understanding of him that had grown out of her evidently long-standing interest. The essay succeeds because Moore's superb description recreates both the sculpture itself and the awe she experienced in seeing the sculpture. The essay succeeds on yet another level because of the skill with which Moore presents such diverse observations and makes all of them operate simultaneously.

Moore's allusive method developed out of her habits of eclectic reading and meticulous recording. Her essays thus vary tremendously in style according to the text she is considering and the allusions she includes. When the text is a written one and when Moore weaves lengthy quotations from that text into her own sentences, the essays become exercises in imitative form. This is quite the opposite of the demuring politesse that some critics see in Moore. Moore's reviews of Wallace Stevens's *Harmonium* and Gertrude Stein's *The Making of Americans* illustrate her method well. Moore's review of *Harmonium*, "Well Moused, Lion," contains on one level the evaluations and comments one would expect in any review of a new book of poetry—descriptions of the poet's characteristic practices, quotations from the poems themselves, and comments on how the work under review either resembles or differs from the work of related poets. Moore emphasizes Stevens's habitual use of color, his creation of imaginary worlds, and his experiments with syntax. She does so, however, with her own characteristic allusiveness and indirection. Stevens's use of color can be best understood in terms of Balzac's claim that he was indifferent toward money unless he could have it "in heaps or by the ton." [13] Moore goes on to discuss Stevens's syntax in terms of Shakespeare's and to compare Stevens's work with that of Oscar Wilde, Rousseau, and Hebrew poetry. While these references indicate Moore's eclecticism, they are also techniques common to any review of poetry. When it comes, however, to quoting from the poems themselves, Moore's imitative form emerges. Her descriptions of Stevens's "riot of gorgeousness" and "clash of pigment" become her own splashes of colorful prose.

Moore's style remains her own but at the same time mimes that of Stevens in its colorful excess. In fact, Moore's sentences flow so smoothly into the embedded and offset quotations borrowed from Stevens that her own words and his nearly become indistinguishable:

> One is met in these poems by some such clash of pigment as where in a showman's display of orchids or gladiolas, one receives the effect of vials of picracarmine, magenta, gamboge, and violet mingled each at the highest point of intensity:
>
>> In Yucatan, the Maya sonneteers
>> Of the Caribbean amphitheatre
>> In spite of hawk and falcon, green toucan
>> And jay, still to the nightbird made their plea,
>> As if raspberry tanagers in palms,
>> High up in orange air, were barbarous.
>
> One is excited by the sense of proximity to Java peacocks, golden pheasants, South American macaw feather capes, Chilcat blankets, hair seal needlework, Singalese masks, and Rousseau's painting of banana leaves and alligators. We have the hydrangeas and dogwood, the "blue, gold, pink, and green" of the temperate zone, the hibiscus, "red as red" of the tropics.
>
>> . . . moonlight on the thick, cadaverous bloom
>>
>> That Yuccas breed . . .
>> . . . with serpent-kin encoiled
>> Among the purple tufts, the scarlet crowns.
>
> and as in a shot spun fabric, the infinitude of variation of the colours of the ocean:
>
>> . . . the blue
>> And the colored purple of the lazy sea,
>
> the emerald, indigos, and mauves of disturbed water, the azure and basalt of lakes; we have Venus "the centre of sea-green pomp" and America "polar purple." Mr. Stevens' exact demand, moreover, projects itself from nature to human nature. It is the eye of no "maidenly greenhorn" which has differentiated Crispin's daughters; which characterizes "the ordinary women" as "gaunt guitarists" and issues the junior-to-senior mandate in Floral Decoration for Bananas:
>
>> "Pile the bananas on planks.
>> The woman will be all shanks
>> And bangles and slatted eyes."   (85)

Later in the review, when Moore praises Stevens's mastery of tone of voice, that ability "to set down words in such a way as to admit of no interpretation or accent but the one intended," she alters her own style to match his. From the quick, colorful phrases with which she had described Stevens's splashy use of color, Moore elongates her sentences in order to introduce his description of "The Wooden ascents / of the ascending of the dead." Her own sentences imitate Stevens's circuitous progress. "One has the effect," Moore explains, "of poised uninterrupted harmony, a simple appearing, complicated phrase of symmetry of movements as in figure skating, tight-rope dancing, in the kaleidoscopically centrifugal circular motion of certain mediaeval dances" (90).

The same practices of eclectic references, lengthy quotations, and imitative form influence Moore's treatment of Gertrude Stein's *The Making of Americans*. The effect, of course, is quite different. Moore admired Stein's dense repetition and begins her review by differentiating Stein's eight-volume, 925-page novel from other "extra-ordinary interpretations of American life." [14] Typically, Moore accomplishes this task by using Stein's own description of the novel as " 'not just an ordinary kind of novel with a plot and conversations to amuse you, but a record of decent family progress respectably lived by us and our fathers and our mothers, and our grandfathers and grandmothers' " (153). Just as the Stevens review contains the elements common to any responsible review of poetry, the Stein review includes basic information about the novel's plot and style and about its relation to or difference from similar works. It also mimes Stein's prose style. The effect, predictably, is strikingly different from that of the Stevens review. Moore's syntax suggests the simplicity, the patterned repetition, and the curiously flat emotion in Stein's prose:

We have here a truly psychological exposition of American living—
an account of that happiness and of that unhappiness which is to
those experiencing it, as fortuitous as it is to those who have an
understanding of heredity and of environment natural and inevitable. Romantic, curious, and engrossing is this story of "the old
people in a new world, the new people made out of the old." There
are two kinds of men and women Miss Stein tells us, the attacking
kind and the resisting each of which is often modified by many complex influences. Mr. Dehning who was of the resisting kind, "never
concerned himself very much with the management of the family's
way of living and the social life of his wife and children. These things
were all always arranged by Mrs. Dehning." Yet "they could each one
make the other do what they wanted the other one to be doing"—
this "really very nice very rich good kind quiet completely successful
a little troubled american man and woman." The unsufficiency of
Alfred Hersland who married Julia Dehning, is shown to be largely a
result of his mother's anonymity, of incompetent pedagogy, of spoil-

ing, and of his father's impatient, unconsidering willfulness. The Dehnings were happy; the Herslands were under the impression that they, too, were happy.   (153–154)

Just as Moore's prose in the Stevens essay grew more riotous in order to keep pace with his poetry, here Moore recreates Stein's complex, highly patterned simplicity by writing in similarly patterned sentences.

These two essays, like many others, reveal Moore's intensity of attention and wealth of reference. They also show the method she had developed for paying homage to authors whose work she admired. Just as Moore believed that ignoring a work was the most effective means of condemning it, she showed indirectly, through imitative form, why an author deserved notice and what that author had accomplished. This indirection in Moore's criticism undoubtedly contributed to the belief that she was too timid to state her own opinions and to the charge that her essays were merely impressionable. On the contrary, Moore exploits indirection so that imitative form becomes critical commentary. At *The Dial*, Moore used the style she had developed in her early essays to question and to undermine some of the assumptions of early modernism.

3 · *The Dial* as "Aesthetic Equivalent"

BY 1925 Marianne Moore had established her reputation as a poet, as a reviewer, and as a member of the elite *Dial* group of writers. When Scofield Thayer decided to resign as that magazine's editor but to continue to sponsor it financially, he asked Moore to succeed him. Moore accepted the position and soon found it to be a full-time undertaking. The editorship pushed Moore into a public role and brought her both praise and condemnation. Undoubtedly, part of the condemnation grew out of discomfort with Moore's inalterable reserve. Indeed, the *Dial* archives sometimes read like comic parodies of style between Moore's eloquence and Pound's ravings, Hart Crane's ire, Cummings's word play, and the assorted anxieties of any number of potential contributors. Just as surely as she was eloquent and polite, Moore was a heavy-handed editor. Her suggestions for revisions outraged contributors as different from one another as Bertrand Russell and Hart Crane. In most cases Moore's suggestions—and she always insisted that they were only suggestions—caused no harm and sometimes led to genuine thanks from the authors in question. On the other hand, Moore's notorious objections to *Finnegans Wake* have aroused universal ire. Literary historians consider the *Finnegans Wake* loss the central event of Moore's editorship and interpret her years at the magazine as the swan song of *The Dial*. Moore critics usually overlook her editorship, treating it as a puzzling if not unfortunate hiatus in her real work. Neither approach recognizes the ironic spirit behind Moore's public facade. Neither takes account of the imitative form and critical principles that Moore had developed in her early essays and went on to refine during her editorship of *The Dial*.

The "official" history of *The Dial* has been written several times.[1] Each study contributes background material about the magazine to which Moore devoted four years of work; and in varying degrees, each offers anecdotes about the magazine's circle of writers. None, however, studies Moore's editorship as a separate entity, and this was of course not their intention. Nor will documenting Moore's day-to-day routine be the subject of this chapter. The record of Moore's editorship as it exists in the

Dial archives shows that she was as opinionated and determined as she was retiring and private. Her definition of American modernism, as it emerges from her editorship, is as untraditional as her prose style is allusive and subtle. Thus, after setting Moore's ideas in perspective and describing her alteration of the editorial policy she had inherited from Scofield Thayer, this chapter will turn to an interpretive reading of Moore's editorship, particularly of the editorial column she wrote for the magazine each month. Those issues and those "Comments" become a showcase for Moore's inclusive taste and for her prophetically postmodern definition of American modernism.

T. S. Eliot's comment on modernism in "Ulysses, Order and Myth," which had appeared in *The Dial* as a book review, helps to set Moore's ideas in perspective. She undoubtedly agreed with Eliot's 1922 proclamation that the central challenge for an artist in the twentieth century is one "of controlling, of ordering, of giving a shape and a significance to the immense panorama of futility and anarchy which is contemporary history."[2] But the issues of *The Dial* that Moore put together show that her interpretation of the task differs from Eliot's in its very essence. Rather than a pessimistic struggle to be engaged in defensively, Moore's editing becomes an optimistic attempt to present and thus enact that pervasive anarchy in each issue of the magazine. Her editorial decisions and each month's "Comment" combine to create what Kenneth Burke might have called the "aesthetic equivalents" of the decade. Those issues confirm, as do Moore's letters and notebooks, that Moore's quaint facade serves as an ironic cover for Moore's prophetically postmodern sensibility. No longer the poet created by John Crowe Ransom in his determination to "reduce [Moore's discontinuity] to a minimum,"[3] Moore emerges from a study of her editorship as an optimistic spirit and a prophetic thinker. Her editorial decisions emphasize the discontinuity and contradiction that her more traditional contemporaries found so troublesome. "Comment," the signature Moore added to each month's issue, goes on to define and to defend "the savage's romance" of twentieth-century American experience.

In accepting the editorship of *The Dial*, Moore inherited a tradition as stately as it was innovative, as austere as it was prestigous. The polemical contemporaries of *The Dial*—*The Little Review, Broom,* and *Blast*—sought to shock their readers, to sweep the dust out of their brains, or to blast them into new levels of consciousness. *The Dial* published many of the same authors but with a more sedate goal: "to turn out each month a flawless journal, . . . to mold every disparate element in American culture into one organic community where men of art were also men of power."[4] Naive and impractical as Thayer's dream may have been, *The Dial* was a remarkable journal—beautifully designed, tastefully illustrated, and meticulously edited. It was also remarkably inclusive, presenting established patriarchs side by side with newly recognized or previously unpublished writers. Thanks to Thayer and J. Sibley Watson's sponsorship, *The Dial* paid its contributors generously. But in wishing to be both democratic and seamlessly inclusive, Thayer found himself pessimistically, if ironically, attempting "to discover what is wrong with the world."[5] In fact, Thayer's disenchantment with the world he wanted to present in *The Dial* appears during his first year as editor when he writes:

> The plaint against modernity has the consoling virtue of being at least as old as antiquity itself, but we cannot help repeating it. Imagine reading
>
>> In Xanadu did Kubla Khan
>> A stately pleasure dome decree
>
> and, turning from the romance and magic of those lines, discovering that in Jamalpur, Bengal, the thirty thousand employees of the Tata Steel Works have gone out on strike. There is a new and separate cruelty about modern society. It informs us of so many things we are helpless to change and of which we would rather remain ignorant. What corruption has come over Jamalpur that it must have steel works, and having steel works, why cannot things be so arranged that we, at least, know nothing of them? (546)

What troubled Thayer was that things could not be so arranged. Marianne Moore's reaction to this same realization provides the key to understanding her editorial sensibility and the wit which informed it. Moore's method and her reinterpretation of *The Dial's* mission is so subtle that it has eluded even Nicholas Joost in his otherwise unassailable history of *The Dial*. In defending what he calls the magazine's attempt to mirror "the pluralist quality of American life," Joost argues that *The Dial* "was a unified artistic entity, constructed with care and . . . making use of the whole orchestra and all of the colors of art."[6] Joost adds that "in this orchestration, 'Comment' played the part of the conductor." His metaphor of conducting is helpful for Thayer's editorship. But since it does not recognize the conflict between Thayer's intention (to mirror the plurality of twentieth-century American life) and his desire to conduct by diminishing that very multiplicity, the metaphor leads to Joost's misreading of Moore's editorship, particularly of her editorial "Comments." By reading with the assumption that "conducting" consisted solely of settling or arguing with the variousness while lamenting its existence, Joost claims that under Moore's hand the column "became less combative in the sense that it usually eschewed the literary controversies of the later twenties" (124). Actually Moore's "Comments" were a far more imaginative and creative undertaking. In them she deliberately reversed the defensive and argumentative tone of the early "Comments." Moore conducted by enacting in her essays the multiplicity and disparateness of the world around her. Moore's essays present judgments, just as Thayer's do, but they are positive judgments that accept and mirror rather than attempt to diminish the fragmentation of the modern world.

Jacques Lacan's theory of the mirror stage of development illustrates the difference between the two approaches and illuminates the method Moore used to create the "Comments" she wrote while editor. Lacan claims that at as early an age as six months a child looking into a mirror recognizes his or her own image as such and identifies with it so thoroughly that the image becomes the source of the infant's secondary identifications. This identification, having taken place at such an early stage in the formation of the child's self-concept, causes the child forever after to strive to become that image. It is a struggle of this sort—Lacan calls it a striving for a "dialectical synthesis"[7]—which Thayer seems to have been engaged in. The mirror image is the modern pluralistic society he wanted to portray in each issue, and the "Comments" are his attempt to achieve that image. Moore's "Comments," on the other hand, directly present her created reflections of the fragmentary plurality she perceived. Her essays are dialectical but show no need for synthesis, and, in fact, subvert the possibility of it, praising disparateness and multiplicity instead. Thus they become her "aesthetic equivalents" of American modernism, a phrase Moore had borrowed from Kenneth Burke. In announcing that Burke had been selected as the recipient for 1928 of the prestigious *Dial* Award, Moore praised him most highly for his belief that an artist's "'moral contribution consists in the element of grace which he adds to the conditions of life wherein he finds himself.'" "As [Burke] has said," Moore added, "'the artist does not run counter to his age; rather, he refines the propensities of his age, formulating their aesthetic equivalents.'"[8]

Moore's style of altering the defensive tone of *The Dial* is consistent with her reserve and subversive indirection. Thus, a history of her editorship provides a context within which to consider her editorial essays. One quickly sees, for instance, that in spite of Moore's own self-effacing accounts of her editorship, she rapidly assumed a position of authority that she used in assembling each issue. The first of the New York experimental poets to have appeared in *The Dial*, Moore soon began publishing reviews and critical essays there, too. She was thus uniquely qualified to "begin work at *The Dial*"[9] when Thayer decided to resign as editor. Aided by a secretary and a managing editor, Moore apparently read every piece of work that was submitted to the magazine. Documentation for the first few months of her editorship exists in her precise, formal letters, which initially asked the advice of J. Sibley Watson, the magazine's other owner, on almost every transaction. These letters quickly become merely informal notations of Moore's editorial decisions to which Watson simply added his approval. Then, far from obediently continuing Thayer's design, Moore began shaping every opinion in the magazine. She sought continued contributions from the established *Dial* authors, William Carlos Williams, and E. E. Cummings; added such diverse writers as Louis Zukofsky, Gertrude Stein, Rainer Maria Rilke, I. A. Richards, George Saintsbury, and Gordon Craig; and very deliberately reintroduced one controversial contributor who had been dismissed.

When Moore wrote Ezra Pound in 1925 asking for critical reviews of E. E. Cummings and Cheever Dunning, she apparently did not know that Pound had argued with *The Dial's* editors concerning the rejection of some of his cantos and that Thayer subsequently wrote Pound terminating his position as Paris correspondent for *The Dial*.[10] A year and a half later, when Moore wrote a second time, she received a scathing reply. Pound claimed that he wouldn't consider giving his journalism to a magazine that threw away his best work, and asked whether she had "ANY knowledge" of his experience with the previous editor.[11] Obviously puzzled, Moore asked Watson for an explanation. In answering, Watson assented, somewhat reluctantly, to Moore's suggestion to publish Pound. He wrote, "With regard to Ezra Pound—if we feel prepared to take whatever he sends I think he can be persuaded to send something. I should be willing to 'take whatever he sends' and always have been, although his work is varied in the extent to which it interests me. Scofield was never anxious to do this and Pound's coolness toward *The Dial* is due to our returning (I think) *Cantos* which he felt we had contracted for. The matter was aggravated by delay."[12] With that explanation, Moore wrote Pound asking for a manuscript. She received no reply but was determined to have his work. Six months later, apparently at Moore's suggestion, Watson cabled: "Wish to offer you *Dial* Award STOP Rule requires contribution from recipient during year STOP If offer acceptable could you send immediately suitable prose or verse Please cable collect."[13] Pound replied the next day in two words, "All right," and soon sent Cantos XXII and XXVII, which appeared, along with the announcement of the award, in January and February of 1928.

Having established her influence in carrying out the mechanics and logistics of editing *The Dial*, Moore soon began to impose her personality on the content and tone of the magazine. While following Thayer's guidelines for maintaining a balance between prose criticism, poetry, fiction, and reproductions of works of art, Moore added a refreshing touch of wit to this controlled arrangement. Her issues consistently emphasize the "disparate elements" of twentieth-century life and thus distinguished her editorial taste from Thayer's. Moore's humor also stands in marked contrast to Thayer's pessimism. It appears, for instance, in her presentation of Charles Trueblood's essay on biography for the August 1927 issue. Trueblood finds fault with the "mature and delicate malice" of Lytton Strachey's interpretive biographies, "which wear somewhat the look of entertainments at the expense of their subjects."[14] Without commenting directly on either Trueblood's essay or Strachey's studies, Moore provided her own bit of ironic entertainment by placing on the facing page a rather funereal Eyre de Lanux portrait of Lytton Strachey sitting in an elaborately carved, claw-footed, crewel-embroidered armchair and peering dourly out through half-closed eyes. His beard reaches nearly to the top of his vest, his right elbow stiffly perches on the arm of the chair, and his chin does not quite rest in his cupped right hand as his exaggeratedly long forefinger curves along the side of his face from his chin to his eyebrows. In yet another instance of this deliberately humorous but unspoken ironic reflexivism, Moore followed her arrangement of Pound's elaborate Guido Cavalcanti translation, complete with his esoteric commentary, with two drawings of American rodeo scenes and William Carlos Williams's prose sketch, "The Venus," which begins, innocently enough, with the question "What then is it like, America?"[15]

Moore obviously enjoyed using such arrangements to set incongruous pieces or opposing points of view against each other. In "Comment" she takes the process one step further. Her independence and her optimistic stance inform her ongoing attempt to define American modernism by subventing the assumptions with which she disagreed. Moore recognized, as William Carlos Williams had explained before she began her tenure as editor, that "modernism is distressing to many who would at least, due to the necessary appearance of disorder in all immediacy, be led to appreciation through critical study."[16] Moore knew not only how to tolerate modernism but also how to enjoy it. Because of that optimism, Moore reversed Thayer's pessimistic stance and defensive attempt to diminish the "disparate elements in American culture." In its place, she offered "Comments," which enact that "necessary appearance of disorder in all immediacy." Thus, at the very peak of modernist attempts to control fragmentation and disorder, Moore consistently argues in favor of inclusiveness. She enacts in prose the variety of American life by incorporating contradictory fragments and unresolvable multiplicity into her essays.

The process is so much a part of Moore's "Comments"[17] that it dictates even their structure. Like much of her poetry, they are difficult, elliptical arrangements, and it is important to understand just how she created them. As if in defense of her creative method, Moore quotes Roger Fry's contention in *Art and Commerce* that "'a really creative design has a certain violence and insistence, a spiritual energy, which is disquieting to people at first sight, however much they come afterwards to like it'" (81, September 1926, 268). The violence of Moore's own creative design was her deliberate confusion of chronological boundaries and her use of fragmentary quotations. One way to understand the method is to recall the image Pound offers in Canto I of the writer at his desk. Surrounded by his books, among them Latin and Renaissance translations of Homer, the artist creates from those sources his own translations of classic texts. Just as Pound's speaker, at a time when he wished to leave one source—Divus's translation of Homer and the appearance there of Antaclea—simply closed that book saying, "Lie quiet Divus" and continued with his own interpretation, so Moore chose the sources she would use and the ways in which she would combine them. Pound chose at will from various translations of Homer, several Anglo-Saxon epics, translations of Ovid, and volumes of Chinese and Renaissance history, superimposing layers of history and disregarding chronology. More eclectic and democratic than Pound, Moore kept at her disposal newspaper clippings, reading notebooks, and apparently the entire contents of her inclusive mind, from which she chose at will to create both poems and critical essays. Like William Carlos Williams, who claimed in 1918 in "Prologue to *Kora in Hell*" that "the sole precedent I can find for the broken style of my prologue is *Longinus on the Sublime*," Marianne Moore also found a useful precedent in Longinus's theory of the "systematic selection of the most important elements, and the power of forming by their mutual combination, what may be called one body. The former process attracts the hearer by the choice of ideas, the latter by the aggregation of those chosen."[18]

Moore defends such fragmentary arrangements and argues in favor of the very idea of collections and anthologies. She complains that "Academic feeling, or prejudice possibly, in favour of continuity and completeness is opposed to miscellany—to music programs, composite picture exhibitions, newspapers, magazines, and anthologies." Admitting that "in what degree diverse subject-matters lend themselves to association, is a question," Moore claims that anthologies present "history recalled as experience . . . as documented *feeling*. Unfamiliar yet actual, like an animal reconstructed from certain bones, they curiously evoke the past, constituting in their chronological sequence, an anthology which results as a skeleton should in being a 'body.'" Moore also claims that in any anthology "a yet more distinct unity is afforded in the unintentional portrait given, of the mind which brought the assembled integers together" (82, May 1927, 450). Her argument is deliberately complex. Collections of miscellany are valuable because each item retains its identity and, contrarily, because those collections simultaneously present, whatever the chronology of the materials, a distinctly unified portrait of the mind that assembled them.

In this treatment of collections and anthologies and in her theory of simultaneity, Moore argues for an historical approach similar to Michel Foucault's antidynastic archaeological view of history, which is neither unified nor organic but rather a series of radical breaks and discontinuities. Edward Said's description of Foucault's undertaking describes Marianne Moore's as well:

> [he] examines *said things (les choses dites)* as they happen before him. His attitude toward the past is that of a spectator watching an exhibition of many events, and what Foucault's reader watches is an exciting intellectual exhibition—and I do not by any means intend this to be a pejorative description. In order to be a spectator, which in this case wrongly implies passivity, there must first be a reordering of documents so that they shed their inertness and become a sort of measurable activity; this re-ordering of texts from the past takes a maximum of intellectual and scholarly energy.[19]   .

Having discovered a creative method so appropriate to her undertaking, Moore used it successfully to define and to defend what she had called in the poem "New York" "the savage's romance" of twentieth-century experience.[20] The effect initially is unsettling; but that was part of Moore's design. "In making works of art," she explained, "the only legitimate warfare is the inevitable warfare between imagination and the medium" (81, December 1926, 536). Moore's medium was "Comment"; and in the warfare to create, she composed essays—sometimes topical, sometimes literary, always elliptical and difficult. Nevertheless, it is possible to reconstruct from them her coherent and persuasive argument for creative imagination and for the mystery and complexity that imagination fosters. This leads ultimately to Moore's affirmation of the multifaceted possibilities, the rough edges, and even the fragmentation of twentieth-century American life.

In the realm of the imagination, Moore's heroes were Blake and Dürer. She admired the precision with which Dürer captured the details of natural phenomena, such as the "eight stranded whales / to look at" and the "water etched with / waves as formal as the scales / on a fish" of "The Steeple-Jack." Even more she respected the freedom with which Dürer "changed / the pine green of the Tyrol to peacock blue and Guinea / gray" (CP, 5). Dürer's ability to portray such imagined scenes with real-world precision became the subject of one of Moore's "Comments":

Dürer's Rhinoceros, Pollajuolo's Battle of the Nudes, and various concepts by Mantegna and by Leonardo da Vinci, have for us that attraction which originality with precision can exert, and liking is increased perhaps when the concept is primarily an imagined one—in the instance of the rhinoceros, based apparently on a traveller's sketch or description. The conjunction of fantasy and calculation is unusual, but many sagacities seem in Dürer not to starve one another. St. Jerome and his beast of burden the lion, in the room with the bottle-glass window lights, the St. Eustacius, a small Turner-like water-colour of the Tyrol in the Ashmolean, tempt one to have favorites, and the eye is promptly engaged by that sensitiveness to magnificence in apparel which gives us the knight's parti-coloured clothing and pointed shoes, the "drowsing elegance of the sugarbag hat," and the little hat "couched fast to the pate like an oyster." Dürer's gifts excited that admiring courtesy of the Italians, we are told; and certain portraits seem to mirror and to gild in the mirroring, Italy's almost finer than Oriental politeness. There is danger of extravagance in denoting as sacrosanct or devout, an art so robust as to include in it that which is neither, but Dürer's separately perfect media do somehow suggest the virtues which St. Jerome enumerates as constituting the "house of cryste"—of which he says in conclusion: "And good perseueraunce nouryssheth theym." His mere journeyings are fervent—to the Dutch coast to look at a stranded whale that was washed to the sea before he was able to arrive; to Bologna to learn as he says, "the secrets of the art of perspective which a man is willing to teach me" and in his several visits to Italy. The secrets of Dürer, however, are not easily invaded, the clearness and simplicity of his signature in the adjusted yet natural housing of the D beneath the mediaevally prominent A, being a subtlety compared with the juxtaposed curves of the modern monogram, the printing of letters backward, or the variously arranged inverting of duplicates. (85, July 1928, 89–90)

Thus, the privacy of Dürer's vision—one "not easily invaded"—gains Moore's final praise.

She found the same combination of fantasy, precision, and privacy in William Blake. Although Moore acknowledges Blake's industry, she attributes his success to the fact that he "could 'see,' and could work—his home being not the age nor the house in which he lived but his mind" (85, July 1928, 90). In a typically synthetic and allusive "Comment," Moore uses Ruskin to begin her treatment of Blake:

"Thousands of people can think for one who can see. To see clearly is poetry, prophecy, and religion all in one." A special kind of seeing, "mental strife," "rapture and labour," are characteristic of few persons indeed, and of no one perhaps to the degree in which they are characteristic of Blake. The incontrovertible actuality of seen impossibilities as he portrayed or told of them, we need scarcely be reminded of—as when in conversation he thus revisualized a fairy's funeral: "I heard a low and pleasant sound and knew not whence it came. At last I saw the broad leaf of a flower move and underneath I saw a procession of creatures of the size and color of green and gray grasshoppers, bearing a body laid out on a roseleaf, which they buried with songs, and then disappeared. It was a fairy's funeral." (84, June 1928, 539)

As though prescribing such fare for the intellectually starved, Moore recommended Lewis Carroll as well: "Unfortunately the romantic book which is insistently advertised as a compendium of fire and flavour, may darken more than it diverts and often it is in the child's book that one finds the really potent principle of which we hear so much." Moore recommended "successive editions of Hawthorne's *Wonder Book*, of *The Wind in the Willows*, *The Little White Bird*, of Padraic Column's 'children's books' and of *Alice in Wonderland*" for "grown people whose patience with [the romantic book] is at an end." The antidote for such mistaken approaches is readily available: "A precision of unlogic in Lewis Carroll, is logic's best apologist—a hypothetically accurate illogical law of cause and effect" (81, August 1926, 177).

Dürer's imagination and Blake's ability to "see" affirm the power of creativity and show that it is inviolable. Each artist convincingly portrays an impossible vision and tempts his audience to believe that it is possible. Exposing this as an illusion, he then establishes the unfathomable mystery of his creation. As a substitute, Moore distrusted "the reliquary method of perpetuating magic"; but she found that an exhibit at the Metropolitan Museum could not diminish the mystery of Dürer's power. Even without accompanying reproductions of Dürer's work, Moore felt that "living energy seemed still to reside in the wood blocks and engraving tools of Dürer's" which were on display there (85, July 1928, 90). While such power is rare, Moore encouraged reverence for and the pursuit of similar illogical mysteries. When the Morris dancers celebrated the rites of spring at the New York Art Center, Moore enjoyed "not knowing the 'purpose' of [the dancers'] wands, bells, blue and cerise ribbons tying the bells to the leg." She insisted, rather, that "there is power in mystery" and that "it is not disappointing not to know the origin of the Morris Dancer or the significance of the handkerchief in either hand" (85, December 1928, 540−541).

Along with her insistence upon mystery as a desirable quality in and of itself, Moore advocated complexity and contradiction, which seem almost her twentieth-century equivalents of mystery. Unlike Thayer, with his distaste for the "new and separate cruelty" of "modern society," Moore insisted on the vivifying possibility of these qualities. Like the exhibit of Dürer's engraving tools, which captured some of the mystery of his awesome power, a chronological display of New York City maps produced a response just as appropriate to its subject:

> Early maps with emphasized shore-lines and rivers have much in common with the modern air-view. Though the photograph may seem as art somewhat "easier" both styles of likeness confer unrealistic distinction, so that New York as foreshortened in a view, taken recently by the Airmap Corporation of America, wears the delicately engraved aspect of a sand-dollar or cluster of barnacles. Our master-production, the Clifford Milburn Holland Vehicular Tunnel, is not visible. In close approach to entrance or exit it is scarcely more perceptible than a wormhole, but pourings of traffic toward Broom Street or from Canal Street indicate sand-adder selfhelpfulness within. (84, April 1928, 360)

Not even blatant irregularities of reproduction diminished the indigenous industry of the city.

Another portrayal of the city, Henry Browne's *New York in the Elegant Eighties,* captured Moore's attention because it offered a chance to perceive the past in the present, to imaginatively recreate that past in terms of the speed and progress of the present:

> How curiously preserved to us both appearances are today with the Columbus Circle monument jacked protectively out of the way of the new subway and peculiar to ships' rats and migratory birds, a residentially changing polarity among our florists, dressmakers, and art dealers. "The charming old home-town feeling" which prevailed in the city as it then was—that city between Maiden's Lane and "the goats"—may still be felt by the superstitious among us, in the region about Trinity Church and the streets near Washington Square. The elbow in Broadway caused by the importance of the apple orchard in "an old farm owned by Henry Brevoort," is preserved to us by Mr. Brown, as are various notable contests—the fight to remove women's hats in the theatre, the crusade against wearing feathers, the battle to compel shop-keepers to provide seats for their clerks. (82, March 1927, 269–270)

What caught Moore's attention in all of these exhibits was an imaginative view of twentieth-century changes, "accreted," as she had described the process, onto a New York where "we need the space for progress." Thus, she disagreed with a writer who boasted "that Europe wasted her time for many thousands of years and that this is the source of her inexhaustibility and fertility—that America's predilection for huge dimensions, for speed and success, is corrupting the world" (81, October 1926, 357). Instead, Moore admits to a wide variety of American qualities without reservation or apology:

> The brittle, brilliant character of life today is varingly exposited. Speed and sport are, it would seem, indigenous to this country. We have the canoe, but ignore the punt and one could inspect the craft belonging to any American yacht-club without finding as a name, the continually approved *Pas Pressé*. We are accustomed in America to admitting that "the prosperous, good-looking domineering woman is a very attractive being." Our most presentable young people seem to share in the attitude of haste, and are accused of irreverence, ingratitude and flippancy. We are, however, encouraged to suspect beneath the mannerism of quick self-sufficiency, a root of seriousness. (80, March 1926, 265)

Moore recognizes that this contradiction, this two-sided opinion of progress, is not a twentieth-century invention. She found precedent for similarly conflicting points of view in an earlier period of American life and uses the discovery to further her exploration of American modernism:

> There is much in life and there is much in art that is not productive of complaisance. One enjoys a sense of magnanimity in George Washington's dismounting to assist a stranger to right an overturned carriage, and denies implication in the slave auction—in the "sickly" creature's going for little and the "good" one's selling for more; but both incidents are really ourselves and are in the eye of honesty to be verified. (81, September 1926, 267–268)

Moore's comments exhibit her inclusive point of view. While she opposed complacency or blind denial of our faults, she also opposed those who responded to the inevitable truth with pessimism. In arguing for an inclusive yet positive attitude in the search for self-definition, Moore offered Emerson's observation in "The American Scholar" as though it were her own: " 'We, it seems, are critical. . . . We cannot enjoy anything for hankering to know whereof the pleasure consists; we are lined with eyes; we see with our feet; the time is infected with Hamlet's unhappiness' " (80, March 1926, 266). Unlike those who, infected with unhappiness and ill at ease with the modern world, might yearn for a return to past simplicity, Moore rejects such romantic notions. She welcomes the twentieth century as an age "of curiosity, of excursiveness and discursiveness" (80, April 1926, 355). She made this point forcefully in her May 1929 "Comment," where she argues in favor of accepting unresolvable contradiction, even when some of it is not entirely pleasant. Her subject is, once again, untraditional and unexpected.

A devoted fan of the circus, Moore visited the Ringling Brothers Barnum and Bailey show twice each year when it came to New York. The "Comment" that she wrote after one of those excursions conveys how much she enjoyed the imaginative escape offered by the circus, but it does not deny some of the show's offensive qualities either. The piece becomes Moore's appreciation and enactment of the three-ring variety and simultaneity of experience that a circus offers. Remarking upon the ubiquitous gilded wagons and hollow music of the circus, Moore adds that the "purity of the new [Madison Square] Garden affords a less likely background than the dingy teacanister aspect of the old one" (86, May 1929, 450). She warns that "where there is much to see, worth is in danger of being overlooked," and acknowledges that "the pain of seeing a bear ride a bicycle may outweigh the pleasure of seeing six little black dogs clown the manoeuvres of Hermann Hesse's six black stallions from Hungary." Nevertheless, Moore finds a pleasant confusion inherent in "the tumblers' fondness for meeting the feet with the hands and resting quadruped-wise, the stomach side in the customary position of the back." In the midst of the Alexander Calder–like riot of visual delight, which Moore captures in her busily ornate prose style, she also argues for the possibility of simultaneous but contradictory perceptions: "Rashness and regality may not be teaching us anything; animals should not be taken from their proper surroundings, and in staging an act the bad taste of patrons should not be deferred to; but apparently this medicinally mingled feast of sweet and bitter is not poisonous; it is not all aconite" (86, May 1929, 450).

This optimism without romantic escape and this double perspective appear throughout Moore's work. As editor of *The Dial*, she used those interests to emphasize the discontinuity and contradiction that so many of her contemporaries wished to diminish. In this undertaking, Moore found a kindred spirit in William Carlos Williams. Moore's essay on Williams, "A Poet of the Quattrocento," appeared in *The Dial* during Moore's editorship and affirms Williams's treatment of the rough edges, the fragmentation, and most of all the multifaceted possibilities of American life. The essay also helped to further Moore's editorial goal. She begins by recalling that Ezra Pound had predicted that "there could be 'an age of awakening in America' which would 'overshadow the Quattrocento'" and that Pound had praised in Williams "'the absolute conviction of a man with his feet on the soil, on a soil personally and peculiarly his own. He is rooted. He is at times almost inarticulate, but he is never dry, never without sap in abundance'" (82, March 1927, 213). In developing her own evaluation of Williams, Moore turns, ironically enough, to Henry James's conviction that young people should "'stick fast and sink up to their necks in everything their own countries and climates can give.'" It is the up-to-the-neck immersion in all things American and modern that Moore praises in Williams and values herself. His view is as inclusive and as optimistic as the one Moore herself had formulated and promoted during her editorship. Williams earns Moore's admiration, thus, because his "topics are American" and because he is "essentially not a 'repeater of things second hand.' . . . That which to some is imperceptible, is to him the 'milligram of radium' that he values" (214–215). Moore continues her praise of Williams, repeating in the essay a quotation she had praised six years earlier in her review of *Kora in Hell:* "'Where does this downhill turn up again? Driven to a wall you'd put claws to your toes and make a ladder of smooth brick'" (215).

Trying to meet the challenge rather than denying or ignoring it gains Moore's praise here and becomes central to one of her poems about meeting the present-day world head-on and without regrets. At ease in "the savage's romance" of her adopted city, Moore enjoyed New York's twentieth-century complexity because it could not be tamed or diminished. In her poem "New York," she explained the attraction of that twentieth-century "center of the wholesale fur trade" by means of a long series of negatives:

It is a far cry from the "queen full of jewels"
and the beau with the muff,
from the gilt coach shaped like a perfume-bottle,
to the conjuncture on the Monongahela and the Allegheny,
and the scholastic philosophy of the wilderness.   (CP, 54)

Neither excessively cultivated nor as isolated at the farthest outpost of commercial trade as Pittsburgh (the real junction of those two rivers and Moore's home at one point) had been in earlier days, Moore's America—and New York, its symbol—remains ineffable:

It is not the dime-novel exterior,
Niagara Falls, the calico horses and the war canoe;
it is not that "if the fur is not finer than such as one sees others wear,
one would rather be without it"—
that estimated in raw meat and berries, we could feed the universe;
it is not the atmosphere of ingenuity,
the otter, the beaver, the puma skins
without shooting-irons or dogs;
it is not the blunder,
but "accessibility to experience."   (54)

Ironically, then, Henry James, Moore's "characteristic American,"[21] once again helps to define contemporary American experience. Open to that experience, Moore sought to capture it in *The Dial*. Her inclusive stance presented the "aesthetic equivalent" of the complex world she lived in. Her subjects and her synthetic prose style are difficult and curious for present-day readers, but the magazine she edited yields, as she knew anthologies could, an "unintentional portrait" of the mind that assembled those issues and wrote those "Comments." A playful rather than a defensive spirit animates that consciousness and stands in sharp contrast to the more familiar image of the accomplished but tame and unimaginative technician. The difference between these two Marianne Moores suggests that the obedient one is the product of what Frederic Jameson calls "the always already read." Apprehended, as Jameson put it, "through sedimented layers of previous interpretations, or . . . through the sedimented reading habits and categories developed by those interpretive traditions,"[22] Marianne Moore has become inseparable from the critical fiction that sought to reduce her discontinuity to a minimum. While one cannot entirely escape from the parameters of "the always already read," Moore's editorship of *The Dial* helps to explode that critical fiction and reveals her humorously ironic sensibility. Moore's poetry exhibits that sensibility at work.

PART TWO ▪ Cultural Combat

4 ▪ "A Reality of Her Own Particulars"

*As much as all imagination does cluster
around fiction, it is also true that all
belief does cluster around another form
of story, history.*

Charles Olson,
The Special View of History

LIKE THE ODOR of the tansy flower, so constant in Charles Olson's child-hood memories of Gloucester that he "didn't know it was / tansey," [1] Marianne Moore's rhetoric has been pervasively inscribed on a number of contemporary critics and critical theorists. In those texts, she occupies a position as ambiguous and undefined as that of the "fellow guests be-side the food, sharing it," which J. Hillis Miller describes in "The Critic as Host" when he attempts to make sense out of "the asymmetrical rela-tionship of critical text to poem." [2] Strangely enough, the unconscious inscriptions of Moore come closer than some formal studies of her work to capturing the imagination and sensibility that pervade her work. This chapter thus begins by exploring the ways in which Moore's rhetoric of the imagination has been unconsciously or marginally inscribed on the works of contemporary critical theorists. The second section of this chap-ter traces these inscriptions back to Moore's appearances in the work of her contemporaries, Wallace Stevens and William Carlos Williams. Moore's essays and poems help these poets to develop their own theories of the imagination. A third section turns to Moore's own comments on the imagination, including her use of Stevens and Williams. Needing nei-ther escape nor destruction, Moore shows that everyday reality, observed and recorded in minutely accurate detail, can be the springboard for limitless imaginative creation.

Words on the Page: Moore's Rhetoric Inscribed

Even the unexamined appropriations of Moore retain shadows of the excitement her contemporaries felt when they first encountered her work. The path of those shadows is circuitous, but it leads eventually to a dis-covered Marianne Moore. One begins with Moore's presence in the work of contemporary critical theorists, then examines the earlier in-stances of such borrowings, and concludes by rereading Moore herself. In her present appropriated incarnation, Moore provides epigrams or pithy quotations that help her critical hosts [3] to support their assertions about other modern or postmodern authors. Those appearances lead back to the poems from which the quotations were taken. Even then, Moore exists not as herself but as a projection of the critical and imaginative fictions and poetic constructs of her contemporaries. At this point, Moore's shadowy presence all but dissolves. For instance, the essays by William Carlos Williams and Wallace Stevens about Marianne Moore become Rorschach tests that reveal more about these two writers than they do about their subject. Williams sees in Moore the disjunctive qualities that define his own work. Stevens finds an entirely different yet equally extraordinary Marianne Moore, one who bears an uncanny relationship to Wallace Stevens.

Moore's own work, however, turns those readings back upon themselves. It shows, for instance, that, as Marjorie Perloff has argued, "the poetics of indeterminacy"[4] can be both powerful and desirable. Like Frank Lentricchia, whose description of life "after the New Criticism" shows that "temporally and culturally uncontaminated ideal meaning"[5] has ceased to be a desirable goal, Moore shows that escapist fictions are neither efficacious nor necessary. Out of that indeterminacy and in place of those fictions, Moore creates what Wallace Stevens, more accurately than he recognized, has called "a reality of her own particulars."[6] Moore's reality, composed of the particulars her reading, her observations, and any fragments of experience that seemed significant, is an inclusive rather than a defensive or an escapist creation. In formulating that reality, Moore calls into question typically modernist attempts to transform or transcend the complexity and the sometimes frightening chaos of the twentieth century. In doing so, Moore presents a negatively capable response that is, very deliberately, *not* an imaginative fiction. Her poems offer an unflinching history of whatever she perceived.

Getting to the history that Moore created requires first seeing the appropriations of her ideas on the imagination. Self-serving though those appropriations may be, they need not necessarily be disregarded or disproved. In fact, such borrowings find precedent in an earlier rewriting of critical history. Frank Lentricchia notes, for instance, that during "the vogue of Wallace Stevens in the 1960s," Frank Kermode played a gracious host to Stevens by appropriating the poet to prove his own critical points. Thus, Stevens's presence in *The Sense of an Ending* becomes an unspoken tribute to the poet's pervasive influence and his timely appeal:

> To what extent Kermode's themes and biases are controlled by the
> poetics of Wallace Stevens is perhaps best attested to by the absence
> in *The Sense of an Ending* of any substantial, frontal discussion
> of Stevens, himself. The poet is present in a closing quotation—
> Kermode gives him the last words of the book. But most tellingly he

is present in the book's texture and rhythm, in words and phrases from his poems and essays which Kermode repeatedly and skillfully weaves into his sentences at key points in the argument. Stevens need no longer be confronted directly because, Kermode appears to have assumed, by 1967 his poetic theories and the very tone of his thought are givens. (*After the New Criticism*, 31)

Lentricchia welcomes Kermode's appropriation of Stevens because of its convincing but "unspoken purpose of radically undermining [Northrup] Frye's premises" of "aesthetic isolationism" (32). In support of Kermode, Lentricchia emphasizes Stevens's "critical self-consciousness which incessantly subverts and dismantles his fictions and shows them for what they are: 'intricate evasions of as'" (32). Lentricchia then goes on to secure Stevens a place in the now desirable postspatial world of postmodernism. Against what he calls "Frye's dominant theme . . . the celebration of the potentially unqualified freedom of the mind's structuring capacities," Lentricchia places his own reading of Stevens:

Stevens' dominant theme is the stubborn independence, the final freedom of being from mind and the priority of natural existence over consciousness. As he puts it in "The Connoisseur of Chaos": "The squirming facts exceed the squamous mind. . . ." Stevens' poetics is a two-term system where fiction and reality engage in endless and complex play in which one term, while open to qualification by another, always successfully resists subsumption by its opponent. So that if Frye's mythic structures are perfectly "closed" to existential reality, then Stevens' fictions would appear to be "open"—which is a way of saying that Frye's myths are spatially isolated, while Stevens' fictions participate in and are subject to the flowing of time. (24)

Although Lentricchia does not use Marianne Moore directly, the argument he uses for Stevens is correct for her as well. Moore's poems show the desirability and expose the insufficiency of imaginative fictions. They refuse to fulfill the expectations that she carefully nurtures in her readers. Throughout the process, Moore remains resolutely inscrutable. Even her critical comments contradict each other with conscious impunity. She praises Stevens for his excellent control of subtle rhyme and complex rhythm; she also writes that "William Carlos Williams objects to urbanity—to sleek and natty effects—and this is a good sign if not always a good thing."[7] In Moore's poetry, these two qualities—technical excellence *and* the rejection of such "sleek and natty effects"— exist side by side, much to the consternation of her readers. Fully aware of this response, Moore describes in "An Octopus" the critical reception which follows from her practice:

It is self-evident
that it is frightful to have everything afraid of one;
that one must do as one is told
and eat rice, prunes, dates, raisins, hardtack, and tomatoes
if one would "conquer the main peak of Mount Tacoma,
this fossil flower concise without a shiver,
intact when it is cut,
damned for its sacrosanct remoteness—
like Henry James "damned by the public for decorum";
not decorum, but restraint;
it is the love of doing hard things
that rebuffed and wore them out—a public out of sympathy with
    neatness.   (CP, 75–76)

While these lines predict the reception likely to follow such decorum, Moore elsewhere goes on to explain that profound emotion lies behind such restraint. In her essay "Feeling and Precision," for example, Moore begins by arguing that "feeling at its deepest—as we all have reason to know—tends to be inarticulate. If it does manage to be articulate, it is likely to seem overcondensed, so that the author is resisted as being disobliging or arrogant" (Pred, 3). Nevertheless, Moore explains, one must continue with efforts one believes in. "Fear of insufficiency is synonymous with insufficiency, and fear of incorrectness makes for rigidity. Indeed, any concern about how well one's work is going to be received seems to mildew effectiveness" (11).

Moore's work was received as often with puzzlement and outrage as it was with praise, and its curious indirection seems to be the cause of her present shadowy inscriptions. For instance, she explains the unusual specificity of her own poems by quoting from the work of her fellow poets:

William Carlos Williams, commenting on his poem "The Red Wheelbarrow," said, "the rhythm though no more than a fragment, denotes a certain unquenchable exaltation"; and Wallace Stevens, referring to poetry under the metaphor of a lion, says, "It can kill a man." Yet the lion's leap would be mitigated almost to harmlessness if the lion were clawless, so precision is both impact and exactitude, as with surgery; and also in music, the conductor's signal, as I am reminded by a friend, which "begins far back of the beat, so that you don't see when the down beat comes. To have started such a long distance ahead makes it possible to be exact. Whereas you can't be exact by being restrained." When writing with maximum impact, the writer seems under compulsion to set down an unbearable accuracy; and in connection with precision as we see it in metaphor, I think of Gerard Hopkins and his description of the dark center in the eye of a peacock feather as "the colour of the grape where the flag is turned back": also his saying about some lambs he had seen frolicking in a field, "It was as though it was the ground that tossed them"; at all events, precision is a thing of the imagination . . . (3–4)

Moore takes that precision—both of technique and of observation—and makes it the criterion by which she evaluates the poetry of her contemporaries. Thus, in "There is a War That Never Ends," she identifies the source of the indeterminacy that Marjorie Perloff admires in William Carlos Williams's poetry and the "two-term system" that Frank Lentricchia admires in Wallace Stevens's fictions, one that "make[s] fact what we want it to be" (Pred, 37). Moore's use of particulars to create her own negatively capable history and thus to deny that an escapist fiction can take its place pervades her work, but it has understandably escaped notice even while it has been inscribed on many critics. Forever allusive, Moore offers seamless poetry and prose, the majority of which is borrowed. In many instances, one can barely tell where her own ideas begin and end. Ironically, though, the frequency with which Moore has begun to appear, however indirectly, in contemporary discussions of postmodern literature and critical theory now makes it possible to discover the ways in which Moore anticipates postmodern thought.

Geoffrey Hartman's *Criticism in the Wilderness,* his apologia for philosophic or continental as opposed to practical Anglo-American criticism, is a good place to begin. Moore emerges from this study, along with William Carlos Williams, as a prototypically American "spring cleaner." This spring cleaning was so successful, reports Hartman, that "since then we have not gotten tired of hearing about the American Sublime, its capaciousness, spaciousness, greatness, newness; its readiness to take on experience and remain sublime."[8]

Ten years before Hartman, Denise Levertov had explored the quest for the American Sublime, including Moore's role in that effort. In Levertov's work, Moore's presence is less conscious, more automatic than in Hartman's. Levertov borrowed Proust's phrase to criticize the mistaken "documentary realism" of poets who imitate the style but fail to capture the spirit of William Carlos Williams: "What Williams said about the American idiom, about the necessity, for a live poetry, of drawing upon the diction and rhythms of the vernacular; and what he did himself, both in that respect and in revealing the neglected worlds that lie about us, has been appropriated, misunderstood, and banalized by innumerable published and unpublished poets, whether or not they know and acknowledge the source of their practices."[9] Levertov turns to Moore but uses her only indirectly when she points out that Williams himself criticized

Whitman and Sandburg, despite their "homespun 'content.'" He preferred, Levertov explains, the genuine newness of "Poe, Cummings,
Pound, Marianne Moore, none of whom consistently, and some of
whom never wrote in simple imitation, reproduction, of the American
idiom, as understood by some of those who today take Williams's name
in vain in defense of their own banalities" (92).

In *Criticism in the Wilderness,* Hartman develops his thought along
those same lines when he claims that imagination, not mechanics, makes
the difference between simple imitation—what he calls "soap opera"
or "warmed-over Whitman"—and "genuine works of language purification." Hartman asks and then answers what he perceives to be the
key question for American poetry in the twentieth century: "Is the pattern, then, all that different from the familiar one of the old European
codgers, of William Butler Yeats, for instance, who embraced the 'desolation of reality' after the circus animals, his illusions and histrionic atti-
tudes had gone? At the very time Williams is thinking of 'capitalizing'
Barnum, Marianne Moore is 'translating' Old World 'Animal Forms
of Wisdom' in her own way. Her splendor, too, is Menagerie" (119).
Hartman recognizes that Williams's endeavor and Moore's are similar,
but he acknowledges that fact by a curious indirection. His reading
of Williams's "The Red Wheelbarrow" praises the poem's disjunctive
quality, "properly rhythmed, punctuated by the mind pressing against
what it perceives." Hartman goes on to substantiate the importance of
simultaneous precision and disjunction by quoting one of Williams's
own essays: "'A word is a word most," Williams wrote, 'when it is separated out by science, treated with acid to remove the smudges, washed,
dried, and placed right side up on a clean surface. . . . It may be used not
to smear it again with thinking (the attachments of thought) but in such
a way that it will remain scrupulously itself, clean perfect, unnicked, be-
side other words in a parade. There must be edges" (120). Although
Hartman barely identifies it as such, this is Williams describing Marianne Moore's work. The conjunction is apt, since each poet attempts to
startle a reader into accurate perceptions that are free of preconceived
emotional attachments. Thus, in explaining Moore, Williams promotes
himself.

In this presumably unintentional self-promotion, Williams was most
successful; and in *Criticism in the Wilderness* Hartman follows his lead.
Moore's words appear at the margins of his text; but following the manner of Kermode's treatment of Stevens, she is at the heart of his argument. Moore earns the one textual reference I have already discussed
and three quotations. The first serves as Hartman's epigraph for his initial
chapter, "Understanding Criticism," about which he has Moore saying:
"To explain grace requires / a curious hand." She next appears to help

Hartman conclude his fifth chapter, "Purification and Danger 1: American Poetry." In that incarnation, Moore is the heroine of Williams's essays, one who helps us see, as Hartman argues, that "poetic diction once rejected had extraordinary virtues, including its nonnatural character, its lucid artifice, the 'mirror of steel uninsistence' (Marianne Moore) by which it made us notice smallest things and ciphered greatest things, and gathered into a few terms, magical, memorable, barely meaningful, the powers of language" (132). Conveniently enough, Moore moves right along with Hartman to his next chapter, "Purification and Danger 2: Critical Style," where she assists him quite neatly in defending both the validity and the malleability of that slippery Derridian signifier. The incarnation is a new one for Moore, but it suggests the directions in which her work is beginning to be taken:

> This language cannot be accommodated, in Derrida's view, to a single register or level of style. Where Gadamer, claiming to follow both Hegel and Plato, sees language as "fusing horizons" through dialogic exchange, Derrida sets column against column, signifier against signifier, and the act of writing against homogeneous discourse. So the word *Hegel* itself is as substantial as a proper name or signature that seals a document. But *Hegel* is also as light and high-flying as the pun that converts the name into *aigle* and makes it appear as Nietzsche's *Ekel* ("disgust") that soars aloft like vatic bird into a region of pure transparency. A region where "light is speech," as Marianne Moore declares, "speech / and light, each / aiding each—when French" (138–139).

Hartman's appropriation of Moore's work shows how pervasively her rhetoric has been unconsciously inscribed on both poets and critics; but she remains, in spite of the appropriation, at the margins of his own text, little more than a clever decoration. In *The Poetics of Indeterminacy*, Marjorie Perloff takes that same perception one step further, but does not yet treat Moore directly. In arguing for the importance of Williams's early rather than his later work, Perloff explains that the poet admired not escapism but a liberating free play of the imagination. She quotes from *Spring and All* to illustrate her point: ". . . the writer of imagination would attain closest to the conditions of music not when his words are dissociated from natural objects and specified meaning but when they are liberated from the usual quality of that meaning by transposition into another medium, the imagination" (113). Perloff then traces Williams's search for methods of achieving that imaginative transport. The complex line of influence "bears the imprint not only of Apollinaire's aesthetic but also of Dada improvisations, of Gertrude Stein's poetry and fiction, and of Rimbaud's *Seasons in Hell* and *Illuminations*, portions of which had appeared for the first time in English translation in the 1920 *Dial"* (110). Inevitably and quite appropriately, Williams turned what he had learned from Apollinaire into a comment on Marianne Moore. Perloff recognizes that Moore's work played the role of catalyst in Williams's perceptions. Quoting from the same paragraph of the same essay that Hartman uses to explain Williams, Perloff does the same; but she clearly acknowledges Moore's role. Perloff's point is that Williams had internalized Apollinaire's validation of an art that was "as abstract as possible and relying 'a good deal on mathematics'" (112). According to Williams, Moore was already writing that mathematical abstraction as poetry: "In a 1925 essay on Marianne Moore, Williams notes: 'A course in mathematics would not be wasted on a poet or a reader of poetry, if he remembered no more from it than the geometric principle of the intersection of loci: from all angles lines converging and crossing establish points'" (113). Here Perloff both inscribes and names Moore's presence. The progression has been gradual and, even in Perloff's treatment of Moore, marginal. Nevertheless, the critics who employ Moore's rhetoric have begun the process of dis-covering the poet who was admired by her contemporaries, contemporaries as different from one another as were Ezra Pound and T. S. Eliot, William Carlos Williams and Wallace Stevens, and Gertrude Stein and Kenneth Burke.

Shards of the Critics: The Use and Abuse of Moore

These present-day inscriptions of Moore's rhetoric find precedent in the work of Moore's contemporaries, specifically William Carlos Williams and Wallace Stevens. Those poets used Moore much more directly than do contemporary critical theorists, and their appropriations are more openly polemical. The Rorschach test of Moore's poetry served for her contemporaries as the source of a number of provocative essays—so provocative that they have nearly eclipsed the poetry itself. Thus, when present-day critics treat the essays of Williams and Stevens, they are often inadvertently discussing Moore as well. But Moore seems to have been forgotten. Nevertheless, the essays written by Stevens and Williams about Moore remain among the best readings her work has received. The similarity at the heart of the poetry of Williams, Stevens, and Moore is their shared interest in the power and in the limits of imagination. With this in mind, it is possible to identify Stevens's and Williams's appropriations of Moore's words and to reconstruct from the shards of that rhetoric her own theory of the imagination. Moore's theory of the imagination is less joyously destructive than the one Williams developed and less drawn toward escape than that of Stevens. In borrowing Moore's ideas, each of these two poets makes his own interest primary. Their ideas of and interests in the imagination are quite different. Thus, their borrowings present two quite different Marianne Moores.

A short passage from Williams's "Prologue to *Kora in Hell*" captures his sense of the imagination, especially when the passage is read in the context of the one preceding it. The two of them appear in the original text as follows:

> VI. No. 1. A fish swimming in a pond, were his back white and his belly green, would be easily perceived from above by hawks against the dark depths of water and from below by larger fish against the penetrant light of the sky. But since his belly is white and his back green he swims about in safety. Observing this barren truth and discerning at once its slavish application to the exercises of the mind, a young man, who has been sitting for some time in contemplation at the edge of a lake, rejects with scorn the parochial deductions of history and as scornfully asserts his defiance.

> XIV. No. 3. The barriers which keep the feet from the dance are the same which in a dream paralyze the effort to escape and hold us powerless in the track of some murderous pursuer. Pant and struggle but you cannot move. The birth of the imagination is like waking from a nightmare. Never does the night seem so beneficent.[10]

In contrast to this turbulent, emotional scene, Stevens's analysis of the imagination in "The Noble Rider and the Sound of Words" is clearly more intellectual and dispassionate: "The subject-matter of poetry is not that 'collection of solid static objects extended in space' but the life that is lived in the scene that it composes; and so reality is not that external scene but the life that is lived in it" (*Necessary Angel*, 25). Stevens recognizes that violence plays a necessary part in any imaginative creation, but for him it is a productive rather than a frightening struggle. He described the way in which imagination could be employed to confront an age without "a grandeur that was, the rhetorical once." He did so in lines that Moore would soon appropriate for her own means. Comparing imagination to nobility, Stevens called it a force:

> Possibly this description of it as a force will do more than anything else I can have said about it to reconcile you to it. It is not an artifice that the mind has added to human nature. The mind has added nothing to human nature. It is a violence from within that protects us from a violence without. It is the imagination pressing back against the pressure of reality. It seems, in the last analysis, to have something to do with our self-preservation; and that, no doubt, is why the expression of it, the sound of its words, helps us to live our lives. (36)

Thus Stevens's solution is as benign as Williams's was emotional. In his estimation, as stated in "Imagination as Value," "the chief problems of any artist, as of any man, are the problems of the normal . . . he needs, in order to solve them, everything that the imagination has to give" (156).

Ferociously dedicated to her privacy and to her own private ideal of excellence, Marianne Moore developed an equally autographic concept of imagination. Beginning with Williams's comments on Moore and moving to the very different poet that Stevens presents in his treatment of her work reveals the divergent points of view and systems of values from which each poet constructs his image of Moore. In light of those differences, Moore's comments on each of them unmistakably reveal her own priorities as well. They appear even more clearly in her poetry.

Williams begins his 1925 essay entitled "Marianne Moore" with a rather depressing assessment of the present state of criticism. The situation offers him a challenge that he meets more than adequately. It also predicts the appropriations I have identified:

> The best work is always neglected and there is no critic among the older men who has cared to champion the newer names from outside the battle. The established critic will not read. So it is that the present writers must turn interpreters of their own work. Even those who enjoy modern work are not always intelligent, but often seem at a loss to know the white marks from the black. But modernism is distressing to many who could at least, due to the necessary appearance of disorder in all immediacy, be led to appreciation through critical study. (*Selected Essays,* 121)

Without doubt, Williams tried to lead Moore's readers to an appreciation of her work. Not surprisingly, Williams explains himself as well. In the 1918 "Prologue to *Kora in Hell*" Williams had justified his "present fragmentary argument" by claiming that it was deliberate: "By the brokenness of his composition the poet makes himself master of a certain weapon which he could possess himself of in no other way. The speed of the emotions is sometimes such that in thrashing about in a thin exaltation or despair many matters are touched but not held, more often broken by the contact" (*Selected Essays,* 14).

Williams goes on to defend his theory of brokenness by showing that it leads to imaginative discovery:

> Although it is a quality of the imagination that it seeks to lace together those things which have a common relationship, yet the coining of similes is a pastime of a very low order, depending as it does upon a nearly vegetable coincidence. Much more keen is that power which discovers in things those inimitable particles of dissimilarity to

all other things which are the peculiar perfections of the thing in question.

But this loose linking of one thing with another has effects of a destructive power little to be guessed at: all manner of things are thrown out of key so that it approaches the impossible to arrive at an understanding of anything. All is confusion, yet it comes from a hidden desire for the dance, a lust of the imagination, a will to accord two instruments in a duet. (16)

Obviously the "loose linking," the "destructive power," and the "confusion" describe Williams's work as well as Moore's. It is those qualities that led him to read her work as a Rorschach test of his own poetry.

Nevertheless, Williams also recognized the ways in which Moore and her work differed from his own. When he was able to keep both points of view alive, his work captured Moore's spirit and intensity as well as her control. Having known Moore for several years certainly helped Williams to see beyond the surface difficulty of her poems. In "Prologue to *Kora in Hell*," Williams portrays Moore in a roundabout fashion. Part of the effect of his characterization begins in the paragraph preceding it. As a means of concluding his discussion of novelty and creativity in art, Williams turns to the ongoing "enthusiasms" of Marcel Duchamp. The abrupt switch to Marianne Moore is part of Williams's design:

One day Duchamp decided that his composition for that day would be the first thing that struck his eye in the first hardware store he should enter. It turned out to be a pickax which he bought and set up in his studio. This was his composition. Together with Mina Loy and a few others Duchamp and Arensberg brought out the paper, *The Blind Man*, to which Robert Carlton Brown, with his vision of suicide by diving from a high window of the Singer Building, contributed a few poems.

In contradistinction to their South, Marianne Moore's statement to me at the Chatham parsonage one afternoon—my wife and I were just on the point of leaving—sets up a North: My work has come to have just one quality of value in it. I will not touch or have to do with those things which I detest. In this austerity of mood she finds sufficient freedom for the play she chooses. (10)

Williams recognized both Moore's "North" and the intensity that informs her imaginative creations. Recalling that "the only help [he] ever got from Miss Moore toward the understanding of her verse was that she despised connectives" (124), Williams devotes most of his essay on Moore to explaining how disjunctive Moore's poetry could be. At the source of Williams's praise is his admittedly "farfetched" claim that "the sole precedent I can find for the broken style of my prologue is *Longinus on the Sublime*" (3). Nevertheless, he goes beyond that to bring to Moore's endeavor a clarity and specificity of insight that is still helpful. Beginning with an overview, Williams develops a geometric metaphor by means of which he explains Moore's work:

> Good modern work, far from being the fragmentary, neurotic thing its disunderstanders think it, is nothing more than work compelled by these conditions. It is a multiplication of impulses that by their several flights, crossing at all eccentric angles, *might* enlighten. As a phase, in its slightest beginning, it is more a disc pierced here and there by light; it is really distressingly broken up. But so does any attack seem at the moment of engagement, multiple units crazy except when viewed as a whole. (123)

In the remainder of the essay, Williams praises Moore's use of color, her "thrilling" ability to "go on—without connective," and her characteristic rhythm. "She is not," he says, "a Swinburne stumbling to music, but one always finds her moving forward ably, in thought, unimpeded by a rhythm. Her own rhythm is particularly revealing. It does not interfere with her progress; it is the movement of the animal, it does not put itself first and ask the other to follow" (125–126). Completing the paragraph containing the familiar sentence about Moore's practice of "wiping soiled words or cutting them clean out, removing the aureoles that have been pasted about them," Williams demonstrates just how Moore accomplishes that task: "For the compositions which Miss Moore intends, each word should first stand crystal clear with no attachments; not even an aroma. As a crosslight upon this, Miss Moore's personal dislike for flowers that have both a satisfying appearance and an odor of perfume is worth noticing" (128). Williams refers here to Moore's "Roses Only," a poem that has not been reprinted since the 1935 edition of her *Selected Poems*. Throughout the essay, Williams employs terms drawn from physics and geometry to explain the excellence of Moore's composition. Her "local color is not, as the parodists, the localists believe, an object of art. It is merely a variant serving to locate [an] acme point of white penetration" (122). Out of the "really distressingly broken up" quality of "good modern work," Moore makes a "brittle, highly set-off porcelain garden . . . the white of a clarity beyond the facts" (124). Even more so Williams is discussing his own poem, "The Rose," which had appeared two years earlier in *Spring and All*. Thus, the Rorschach test of Williams's "Marianne Moore" essay makes a case for her work that is only partially correct:

The interstices for the light and not the interstitial web of thought concerned her, or so it seems to me. Thus, the material is as the handling: the thought, the word, the rhythm—all in the style. The effect is in the penetration of the light itself, how much, how little; the appearance of the luminous background. . . . There must be edges. This casts some light I think on the simplicity of design in much of Moore's work. There must be recognizable edges against the ground which cannot, as she might desire it, be left entirely white. Prose would be all black, a complete black painted or etched over, but solid.

There is almost no overlaying at all. The effect of every object sufficiently uncovered to be sufficiently recognizable. This simplicity, with the light coming through from between the perfectly plain masses is however extremely bewildering to one who has been accustomed to look upon the usual "poem," the opaque board covered with vain curlicues. They forget, those who would read Miss Moore aright, that white circular discs grouped closely edge to edge upon a dark table make black six-pointed stars. (128–129)

Williams is correct in pointing out that Moore makes her objects "barely recognizable." In doing so, he explains, she achieves a "white clarity beyond the facts," one that survives without *ex machina* props and without "the excuse of 'nature,' of the spirit, mysticism, religiosity, 'love,' 'humor,' 'death,'" (126). Nevertheless, Williams's interest in the manipulations of negative space—as illuminating as it may be for his own poetry—draws attention away from the way in which Moore actually did wipe "soiled words" clean of their habitual emotional attachments. The poem Williams is actually discussing appeared in *Spring and All* after a passage in which he discussed the power of imaginative creation and "the falseness of attempting to 'copy' nature."[11] Williams breaks off from that pursuit—quite abruptly—in order to illustrate what he calls "the modern trend." It is an attempt "to separate things of the imagination from life . . . by using the forms common to experience so as not to frighten the onlooker away but to invite him in" (249).

> The rose is obsolete
> but each petal ends in
> an edge, the double facet
> cementing the grooved
> columns of air—The edge
> cuts without cutting
> meets—nothing—renews
> itself in metal or porcelain—

wither? It ends—

But if it ends
the start is begun
so that to engage roses
becomes a geometry—   (249)

In these lines, Williams uses that geometry to show that "The rose carried the weight of love / but love is at an end—of roses" (249). The poem is clearly the source of his description of Moore's poetry as a "brittle, highly set-off porcelain garden" (*Selected Essays*, 124). Williams separates the rose from its connotations and from the space around it, but he shows that it remains self-sufficient:

Crisp, worked to defeat
laboredless-fragile
plucked moist, half-raised
cold, precise, touching

What

The place between the petal's
edge and the

From the petal's edge a line starts
that being of steel
infinitely fine, infinitely
rigid penetrates
the Milky Way
without contact—lifting
from it—neither hanging
nor pushing—

The fragility of the flower
unbruised
penetrates spaces.
        (*Collected Early Poems*, 249)

This same self-sufficiency appears in Moore's "Roses Only," but not in the geometric terms that Williams has attributed to her. Instead, the poem exemplifies what Williams calls her "burrowing through" and "blasting aside." The result is a rose whose self-sufficiency is more consciously earned, less fragile than Williams's. Moore addresses the roses directly and reprimands them for not recognizing their power:

You do not seem to realize that beauty is a liability rather than
  an asset—that in view of the fact that spirit creates form we
      are justified in supposing
      that you must have brains.   (SP, 42)

Moore also admires the roses as "a symbol of the unit." Out of that she
develops her own variation of the separate existence of the flower as an
object in its own right rather than as a symbol. As that independent object, the rose is

  stiff and sharp,
  conscious of surpassing by dint of native superiority and liking
      for everything
  self dependent, anything an

  ambitious civilization might produce   (42)

But, as Williams recognized in his own poem, the rose's brilliance de-
rives not from its petals, admittedly as Moore puts it, "the without-
which-nothing of / pre-eminence." It is the rose's thorns that keep it
from becoming "a mere / peculiarity." Those thorns, as Moore says, "are
not proof against a worm, the elements, / or mildew; / but what about
the predatory hand?" The rose, like the compositions that Williams admired, has both "brilliance" and "Co-ordination." The difficulty of pos-
sessing it gains Moore's final praise for the flower:

  Guarding the
  infinitesimal pieces of your mind, compelling audiences to
  the remark that it is better to be forgotten than to be remem-
      bered too violently,
  your thorns are the best part of you.   (42)

The passage indicates Moore's intense concern for privacy, and in it
Williams saw the words of a poet who had constructed adequate de-
fenses against the predatory hand of readers governed by habitual reading habits. Williams's geometric analogy for Moore's method of presentation emphasizes her ability to present details in a manner that
defamiliarizes her subject and thus forces readers into new ways of
seeing. Williams's reading is, thus, helpful as far as it goes. It stops, however, with the coincidence of his own interests with Moore's. Williams
does not recognize that Moore wipes the soiled and automatic connotations away from the rose even more convincingly that he had imagined
was possible. Williams's flower is a romantic adventurer that "pene-

trates / the Milky Way." Moore accepts the rose's earthly, inherent contradictions—"Would you not, minus / thorns, be a what-is-this, a mere // peculiarity?"—and makes a universe out of that. The Moore whom Williams presents is thus interesting but not entirely accurate.

At the outset, Wallace Stevens's concern with Marianne Moore's work seems identical to that of William Carlos Williams. Stevens also recognized Moore's ability to make her audience see, but a different sort of seeing concerns him. In "Three Academic Pieces," Stevens claims that "The accuracy of accurate letters is an accuracy with respect to the structure of reality." He adds that "if we desire to formulate an accurate theory of poetry, we find it necessary to examine the structure of reality, because reality is the central reference for poetry" (*Necessary Angel*, 71). Exactly what type of reality concerns Stevens and what he felt a poet must do with it becomes evident in his own Rorschach test, "About One of Marianne Moore's Poems." However, Stevens had begun even earlier to develop those ideas. In "The Noble Rider and the Sound of Words," Stevens argues that the task of the artist is "to discover the possible work of art in the real world, then to extract it" (*Necessary Angel*, 30). He anticipates the objections that might be raised to this technique and argues against them:

> The poetic process is psychologically an escapist process. The chatter about escapism is, to my way of thinking, merely common cant. My own remarks about resisting or evading the pressure of reality mean escapism, if analyzed. Escapism has a pejorative sense, which it cannot be supposed that I include in the sense in which I use the word. The pejorative sense applies where the poet is not attached to reality, where the imagination does not adhere to reality, which, for my part, I regard as fundamental. (30–31)

Stevens clarifies what he means by this fundamental dependence when he examines the way in which Moore manipulates reality in "He Digesteth Harde Yron." "Nowhere in the poem," Stevens notes, "does she speak directly of the subject of the poem by its name." This is the source of Stevens's interest in the poem. In pursuit of fact—the reality of the ostrich that is the subject of Moore's poem—Stevens went one step beyond Moore's elaborate "Notes" for the poem to the *Encyclopaedia Britannica*. Stevens was searching for the core of reality, that "aspect of individuality at which every form of rational explanation stops short" (93). Having first examined Moore's use of Lyly's *Euphues*, Stevens reports that "Lyly repeats the following bit of folk-lore."

> Let them both remember that the Estridge
> digesteth hard yron to preserve his health.

Stevens goes on to cite passages from Moore's poem as well as from the encyclopaedia, all by way of supporting his claim that Moore manipulated fact to create her own reality:

In the second stanza [Moore] says:

> This bird watches his chicks with
> a maternal concentration, after
>   he has sat on the eggs
>   at night six weeks, his legs
> their only weapon of defense.

The *Encyclopaedia Britannica* says of the ostrich:

> *Extremely fleet of foot, when brought to bay the ostrich uses its strong legs with great effect. Several hens combine to lay their eggs in one nest, and on these the cock sits by night, while the females relieve one another by day.*

Somehow, there is a difference between Miss Moore's bird and the bird of the *Encyclopaedia*. The difference grows when she describes her bird as

>   The friend
> of hippotigers and wild
>   asses, it is as
>   though schooled by them he was
> the best of the unifying
> pegasi.

The difference signalizes a transition from one reality to another. It is the reality of Miss Moore that is the individual reality. That of the *Encyclopaedia* is the reality of isolated fact. Miss Moore's reality is significant. An aesthetic integration is a reality. (94–95)

Almost as an apology, Stevens acknowledges the Platonic nature of this assertion and exonerates Moore from any such practice. Her indirection, he explains, "shares in that asceticism . . . only as it may be necessary for her to do so in order to establish a particular reality or, better, a reality of her own particulars" (95). Stevens recognizes that the poem "has an extraordinarily factual appearance," but he finds surprisingly that "it is, after all, an abstraction" (95).

Nevertheless, it isn't an abstraction that Stevens selects to prove his point. Clearly, poetry's ability to offer transport or escape by means of such abstraction is an essential quality in Stevens's system of value. He believes that poetry can and ought to create "a reality adequate to the profound necessities of life today or for that matter any day" (102). But in the case of Marianne Moore, Stevens seems to be arguing against as well as in favor of his claim. For instance, Stevens wants to show that

Moore "irrevocably detaches her [bird] from the *Encyclopædia*" (97). Yet
he cites the following passages to illustrate his point:

> How
> could he, prized for plumes and eggs and young, used
>   even as a riding-
>   beast, respect men hiding
> actorlike in ostrich-skins, with
> the right hand making the neck move
>   as if alive and
>   from a bag the left hand
>
> strewing grain, that ostriches
> might be decoyed and killed!
>
>   ■   ■   ■   ■   ■   ■   ■   ■   ■   ■   ■
>
> whose comic duckling head on its
> great neck, revolves with compass-
>   needle nervousness,
>   when he stands guard in S-
> like foragings as he is
> preening the down on his leaden-skinned back.   (97–98)

Undoubtedly these sketches define the bird beyond the limits of any
encyclopaedia, but they also help Moore to retain rather than to escape
from the reality of the "camel-sparrow" of the poem. This "alert gargantuan / little-winged, magnificently speedy running-bird" has been
spared the extinction that "swallowed up" its near relatives precisely because of its individuality. What Stevens calls its " 'harde yron' of appearance" cannot be effaced. The curious facts and ungainly appearance of
Moore's "camel-sparrow" persist in spite of attempts to appropriate the
bird for vain domestic pursuits:

> The egg piously shown
> as Leda's very own
>   from which Castor and Pollux hatched,
> was an ostrich egg. And what could have been more fit
> for the Chinese lawn it   ▸
>
>   grazed on as a gift to an
>   emperor who admired strange birds, than this
> one, who builds his mud-made

> nest in dust yet will wade
>> in lake or sea till only the head shows.   (CP, 100)

The predatory attempts of would-be possessors to ignore the ungainly and unfathomable qualities of this ostrich succeed, but not entirely.

> Six hundred ostrich-brains served
> at one banquet, the ostrich-plume-tipped tent
> and desert spear, jewel-
> gorgeous ugly egg-shell
>> goblets, eight pairs of ostriches
> in harness, dramatize a meaning
> always missed by the externalist.   (100)

According to Marianne Moore, that meaning is defined thus: "The power of the visible / is the invisible." It is the power which keeps her "remaining rebel . . . the camel-sparrow" alive. Moore's first stanza sets up the boundaries within which she will define that power:

> Although the aepyornis
>> or roc that lived in Madagascar, and
> the moa are extinct,
> the camel-sparrow, linked
>> with them in size—the large sparrow
> Xenophon saw walking by a stream—was and is
> a symbol of justice.   (99)

Moore establishes the "was" as historical fact. Her "Notes" report that "an ostrich plume symbolized truth and justice, and was the emblem of the goddess Ma-at, the patron saint of judges. Her head is adorned with an ostrich feather, her eyes are closed . . . as Justice is blindfolded" (CP, 277). Moore's "is" is more subtle. It is the circumstance that "contradicts the greed that did not wisely spare / the harmless solitaire // or great auk in its grandeur." That justice-by-default of which Moore's ostrich is now a symbol persists in spite of predatory greed, in fact because such predators have been misled by the ungainly outward features of this "alert gargantuan / little-winged, magnificently speedy running-bird." They fail to recognize that "the power of the visible / is in the invisible." It is a meaning "always missed by the externalist."

On this point Stevens misreads Moore, and a digression in his essay shows how and why. In the second of three parts of "About One of Marianne Moore's Poems," Stevens breaks off from discussing Moore's poem to recount his recent visit to the graveyard of an old church. Although moved by the dedication of his hosts to their church, Stevens found the graveyard distressingly barren and bleak:

This was an inclosure of about an acre, possibly a little more. The wall was of limestone about four feet high, weather-beaten, barren, bald. In the graveyard were possibly eight or ten sheep, the color of the wall and of many of the gravestones and even of some of the tufts of grass, bleached and silvery in the hard sunlight. The droppings of the sheep fertilized the soil. There were a few cedars here and there but these only accentuated the sense of abandonment and destitution, the sense that, after all, the vast mausoleum of human memory is emptier than one had supposed. Near by stood the manse, also of limestone, apparently vacant, the upper part of each window white with the half-drawn blind, the lower part black with the vacantness of the place. Although the two elderly men were in a way a diversion from the solitude, there could not be any effective diversion from the reality that time and experience had created here, the desolation that penetrated one like something final. (*Necessary Angel*, 101)

The discomfort Stevens felt when confronted with the blunt facts of that landscape stands in contrast to his reaction shortly thereafter when he viewed an exhibit of decorative books: "The brilliant pages from Poland, France, Finland and so on, books of tales, of poetry, of folk-lore, were as if the barren reality that I had just experienced had suddenly taken color, become alive and from a single thing become many things and people, vivid, active, intently trying out a thousand characters and illuminations" (102).

While Moore found power in the most mundane and unfathomable qualities of the "camel-sparrow," Stevens preferred the transport from reality made possible by the book exhibit. He returns to Moore's poem in the third part of "About One of Marianne Moore's Poems" and interprets the poem according to the preference for escape. Moore creates what Stevens calls "recognizable reality, because, as it happens, she has the faculty of digesting the 'hard yron' of appearance" (103). That power of digesting and thereby transforming would have enabled Stevens to see beyond the sheep droppings to the spiritual qualities that his hosts, the church members, evidently saw and felt. The situation needed imagination or what Stevens in "Imagination as Value" called "the power that enables us to perceive the normal in the abnormal, the opposite of chaos in chaos" (153). The purpose of such transformation, Stevens claims, is to create "a world that transcends the world and a life livable in that transcendence. It is a transcendence achieved by means of the minor effects of figurations and the major effects of the poet's sense of the world and of the motive music of his poems . . . Thus poetry becomes and is a transcendent analogue composed of the particulars of reality, created by the poet's sense of the world, that is to say his attitude as he intervenes and interposes the appearances of that sense" (130).

Marianne Moore interposes her sense, as Stevens recognizes, by placing emphasis upon the imagined irony of the ostrich's point of view toward his captors. However, her ability to keep raw facts in view, to report on so many predatory actions, and to develop her own interpretation out of both sets of facts shows that she does the very opposite of "digesting" outward appearances. Moore's "Notes" set the matter straight in the lines that Stevens himself used in his essay: "The ostrich digesteth harde yron to preserve his health." The bird grows stronger on such self-imposed adversity, and Moore admires that tenacity. Her poem, however, grows stronger not by digesting the "hard iron"—the incontrovertible, contradictory, and sometimes amusing facts of the bird's appearance—but by keeping it visible and by weaving her own story out of and around those facts. Thus, she achieves the desirable, nonpejorative escapism that for Stevens must be a part of poetry, but she also maintains the hard edge of fact that Williams valued so highly.

The Subject on Herself:
Moore as a Theorist of Her Own Imagination

The readings that William Carlos Williams and Wallace Stevens offer of Marianne Moore's work emphasize such divergent qualities and accomplish that task so convincingly that her work might seem, in light of them, hopelessly contradictory and elusive. Nevertheless, the common focus of each of these two poets on Moore's imagination provides a starting point for returning to her own work. In particular, Moore's comments on Stevens's imaginative transformations provide a necessary corrective to his view because they emphasize not escapism and transport in themselves but the violence and power that such imaginative undertakings demand and make possible. In "Conjuries That Endure," Moore calls Stevens "America's chief conjurer—as bold a virtuoso and one with as cunning a rhetoric as we have produced" (Pred, 32). Since such expertise has begun to arouse suspicion, Moore goes on to say that "He has naturally in some quarters been rebuked for his skill; writers cannot excel at their work without being, like the dogs in *Coriolanus*, 'as often beat for their barking / As therefore kept to do so'" (32). But while Moore documents Stevens's skill with rhyme, rhythm, and tone of voice, she saves her highest praise for his imaginative constructions, his ability to show "that imagination and the imaginer are different from images and imagers, from the nature-loving Narcissus who sees only himself in

every pool" (37–38). That ability and Stevens's technical skill combine
to produce what Moore calls "his 'imagination's Latin'—compounded 'of
speech, paint, and music'—[which] enables us to 'see the sun again
with an ignorant eye'" (36). The process involves unusual power, a
power that Moore admires in Stevens's work.

Taking her cue from Stevens's "Poetry is a Destructive Force," Moore
explains in "There Is a War That Never Ends" that "a poet does not speak
language but mediates it, as the lion's power lies in his paws; he knows
. . . that the 'impossible possible' of imagination is so much stronger
than reason that the part is equal to the whole" (37). Here Moore seems
to agree with Stevens's claim that in "He Digesteth Harde Yron" she had
dissolved and transformed fact in favor of the "reality of her own particulars." Clearly Moore enjoys Stevens's "playfulness" and "bravura,"
and she identifies the role they play in his poetry. "Upon the general ma-
rine volume of stalemate is set a parachute-spinnaker of verbiage which
looms out like half a cantaloupe and gives the body of the theme the
air of a fabled argosy advancing" (33). Stevens is, moreover, "a delicate
apothecary of savors and precipitates [whose] method of hints and disguises should have Mercury as consultant-magician, for in the guise of a
'dark rabbi,' an ogre, a traveller, a comedian, an old woman, he deceives
us as the god misled the aged couple in the myth" (34). Moore explains
that Stevens accomplishes this magical transport by means of his "plas-
ter temporariness of subterfuge" (32). In pursuit of that goal, his "af-
firming freedom of mind is involved in 'war that never ends'" (41).

Both the affirmation and the war which Stevens engages in to bring it
about gain Moore's attention in a way that explains her own priorities.
She notes that "in each clime the author visits, and under each disguise,
the dilemma of tested hope confronts him. . . . The protest against the
actualities of experience becomes a protest against the death of world
hope" (35). In those same poems, she adds, "We feel in the detached
method of implication the influence of Plato, and an awareness if not the
influence, of T. S. Eliot. . . . Each has an almost too acute concept of 'the
revenge of music'" (33–34). Although Moore does not define what she
means by that "revenge" and, in fact, clearly admires the skill and the
lighthanded touch that Stevens brings to this "dilemma of tested hope,"
she does not believe that a poet should use the music of his lines or any
other device to "digest" outward reality. She even defends Stevens against
this charge: "Wallace Stevens is as susceptible to sounds as objects were
to Midas's touch. But he does not sophisticate his music" (39). In place
of the transport made possible by such sophistication, Moore privileges
confrontation. She calls it Stevens's engagement in that "war that never
ends." As one example of this power, Moore quotes Stevens in "The

Noble Rider and the Sound of Words": "'as a wave is a force and not the water of which it is composed, which is never the same, so nobility is a force. . . . It is a violence from within that protects us from a violence without. It is the imagination pressing back against the pressure of reality'" (41).

This pressure, which becomes "'the bread of faithful speech,'" is the essential quality that Moore appropriates in her appraisal of Stevens. Thus, although she recognized that his imagination was "a device for evading the world without imagination," she saw in the process a power made possible by means of contained violence. In "Well Moused, Lion," a 1921 *Dial* review of *Harmonium*, she wrote, "Imagination implies energy, and imagination of the finest type involves an energy which results in order 'as the motion of a snake's body goes through all parts at once and its volition acts at this same instant in coils that go contrary ways'" (76, June 1924, 86). Thus, Moore's reading of Stevens's claim for the power of language is more forceful than his own. While Stevens had explained imaginative language as "a violence from within that protects us from a violence without" (*Necessary Angel*, 36), Moore took the violence, made it active, and turned its force outward. It appears in her poetry as "coils that go contrary ways."

This same belief in contraries and in the creative use of violence governs Moore's approach to William Carlos Williams. Not surprisingly, Williams's concerns are closer to Moore's own. Rather than pursuing imagination as an agent of escape, Moore turns her attention to the ways in which Williams explores the imaginative possibilities of topics that are American. She is quite specific on the subject, and "A Poet of the Quattrocento" begins with Henry James: "In his modestly emphatic respect for America he corroborates Henry James's conviction that young people should 'stick fast and sink up to their necks in everything their own countries and climates can give,' and his feeling for the *place* lends poetic authority to an illusion of ours, that sustenance may be found here, which is adapted to artists" (*The Dial*, 82, March 1927, 213).

Emphasizing Williams's rejection of the rush to worship all things European, Moore insists, along with him, that "the very purest works of the imagination may also be found among us. . . . The staying at home principle could not, he is sure, be a false one where there is a vigorous force with buoyancy of imagination" (214). She also notes that Williams has "visited various places and studied various writings and a traveller can as Bacon says, 'prick in some flowers of that he hath learned abroad.' In the main, however, Doctor Williams' topics are American—crowds at the movies . . . the ball game" (214). In contrast to the "revenge of music" that Stevens possessed and Moore accepted but with reservation,

Williams's skill is "his manner of contemplating with new eyes, old things, shabby things . . . The experience ever in encountering that which has been imaginatively assembled is exceedingly new" (214).

Without giving examples, as she so generously does in discussing Stevens's technique, Moore captures the essence of Williams's undertaking: "One sees nothing terrifying in what Doctor Williams calls a 'modern traditionalism,' but to say so is to quibble. Incuriousness, emptiness, a sleep of the faculties, are an end of beauty, and Doctor Williams is vivid. Perhaps he is modern. He addresses himself to the imagination. He is 'keen' and 'compact'" (215). In this imaginative pursuit, Moore acknowledges in "Things Others Never Notice," "the poem often is about nothing that we wish to give our attention to, but if it is something he wishes our attention for, what is urgent for him becomes urgent for us" (Pred, 139). In this call for our attention, there is no question of "digesting" appearances:

> With the bee's sense of polarity he searches for a flower, and that flower is representation. Likenesses here are not reminders of the object, they are it, as in "Struggle of Wings":
>
>> And there's the river with thin ice upon it
>> fanning out half over the black
>> water, the free middlewater dancing under its
>> ripples that move crosswise on the stream. (138)

Nor are there traditional requirements of logic and reason. "His 'venemous accuracy,' if we may use the words used by him in speaking of the author of 'The Raven,' is opposed to 'makeshifts, self-deceptions and grotesque excuses'" (134). Instead there are more exciting qualities: "Struggle is the main force in William Carlos Williams. And the breathless budding of thought from thought is one of the results and charms of the pressure configured. With an abandon born of inner security, Dr. Williams somewhere nicknames his chains of incontrovertibly logical apparent nonsequiturs, rigmarole" (136).

It is easy enough to outline the ways in which Stevens and Williams, the contemporaries with whom Moore shares a common set of aesthetic values, appropriate her work for their own polemic. Moore reciprocates, as I have shown here, but with essays that reveal less about her own priorities than about the poets she has been reading. Thus, while Marjorie Perloff effectively quotes Williams's writing on Marianne Moore to explain his own influence on today's "poetics of indeterminacy," one cannot reverse the process. Almost all of the key passages in Moore's critical essays appear in the form of quotations from the poet she is discussing or from someone else. Her careful documentation is deliberately and most frustratingly circular. Even Moore's comments on imaginative writing in general refrain from explicitly dogmatic statements with infuriating regularity. Her pronouncements sound more like aphoristic puzzles than literary pronouncements. Given such enigmatic declarations as the following ones, it is no wonder that Moore seems to have been appropriated—used and abused—more often than actually read.

You don't devise a rhythm, the rhythm is the person, and the sentence is but a radiograph of personality. (Pred, 3)

Concentration—indispensable to persuasion—may feel to itself crystal clear, yet be through its very compression the opposite, and William Empson's attitude to ambiguity does not extenuate defeat. (Pred, 15)

gusto thrives on freedom, and freedom in art, as in life, is the result of a discipline imposed by ourselves. (Pred, 20)

The thing is to see the vision and not deny it; to care and admit that we do. (Pred, 20)

As circular and enigmatic as these assertions may seem, they are as genuine as any Moore ever made. She repeatedly disavowed any attempt to be unnecessarily complex; and she denied that her compositions, which she refused to call poems, were in any way avant-garde.

Whether or not we give Moore the last word in these matters, she provides us, perhaps unwittingly, with clues to her work. The radiograph divulges the broken style that Williams projected onto her. But it shows that she achieved what he called her "incomprehensibility" through strict control of form. It shows, further, that although her topics were as American as those which Williams promoted, she also fulfilled his challenge that poetry should present "definite objects . . . with no attachments not even an aroma" (*Selected Essays,* 315–316), even more successfully than Williams himself did. In reviewing Williams's *Collected Poems,* Moore identified both his own compliance with and his violation of that dictum. "He is at times almost insultingly specific," Moore admits, "but there is in him—and this must be our consolation—that dissatisfied expanding energy, the emotion, the *ergo* of the medieval dialectician, the 'therefore' which is the distinguishing mark of the artist" (Pred, 139). An additional observation suggests that Moore's title, "Things Others Never Notice," is ironic. Having borrowed the phrase from Williams, Moore goes on to claim that Williams is "drugged with romance" (138). Just as Stevens argued that his own escapism should not carry a pejorative sense, Moore refrains from turning this observation into an accusation against Williams. She is as sincere in complimenting the romantic plea of "Birds and Flowers"—"he has never drawn a clearer self-portrait"—as she is in admiring "'the senseless arrangement of wild things' which he imitates" (139).

While Moore admires Stevens as "America's chief conjurer" and enjoys the fanciful arrangements that Williams makes out of his attention to local minutiae, her own work seems determined to construct the possibility of imaginative escape only so that she can deny with the left hand what her right hand has just finished creating. Certainly, Moore enjoys and ably presents the fragmentary detail, the porcelain garden, and the raw edges of fact that Williams admired. "Complexity," as she says in "In the Days of Prismatic Color," "is not a crime." Her illustration and defense of this observation appears throughout the poetry, particularly when she argues, as Williams does, that such qualities represent American life. One who "'dresses // in New York but dreams of / London,'" will look "somewhat odd" (CP, 103). A better fate comes from realizing with the "zest" of a dedicated baseball fan that "'hope springs eternal in the Brooklyn breast'" (CP, 182). The New York that offered Marianne Moore access to an "accreted" "savage's romance" and the "grassless, linksless, languageless" America of her poems promises adventure and excitement; but not every viewer recognizes this as so. In "England," a poem that is really about America, Moore makes this argument explicitly:

> To have misapprehended the matter is to have confessed that one has
>   not looked far enough.
> The sublimated wisdom of China, Egyptian discernment,
> the cataclysmic torrent of emotion
> compressed in the verbs of the Hebrew language,
> the books of the man who is able to say,
> "I envy nobody but him, and him only,
> who catches more fish than I do"—
> the flower and fruit of all that noted superiority—
> if not stumbled upon in America,
> must one imagine that it is not there?
> It has never been confined to one locality. (CP, 47)

If that search for the local, for "what was originally one's object— / substance at the core" (46), Moore recognizes the possibility of isolation. Like the student who refuses "to be less // than individual," the poet may find himself one who

> renders service when there is
> no reward, and is too reclusive for
>   some things to touch

him, not because he
   has no feeling but because he has so much. (CP, 102)

That surfeit of feeling reinforces Moore's distrust in the efficacy of solutions. "It may be," she explains, "that we / have not knowledge, just
opinions, that we / are undergraduates, / not students." Nevertheless,
within those limits there is potential.

                    With us, a
school—like the singing tree of which
the leaves were mouths singing in concert—
      is both a tree of knowledge
and of liberty,—   (101)

Moore's comment presents a striking contrast with the one that William
Carlos Williams develops out of the same circumstances and by means of
the same image. After describing a parched "America some years after its
original," he indicates the degree to which his loss of romantic illusion
has left him feeling vulnerable: "The art of writing is to do work so excellent that by its excellence it repels all idiots but idiots are like leaves
and excellence of any sort is a tree when the leaves fall the tree is naked
and the wind thrashes it till it howls." [12]

Williams's American writer obviously suffers after his necessary loss
of romantic illusion. Moore inhabits neither this extreme of howling
rage nor the assurance of Williams's later serene claim that "love and
imagination / are of a piece / swift as the light // to avoid destruction." [13]
Instead, the excellence and the power of Moore's created "reality of her
own particulars" comes from the precision with which she insists upon
its limitations. In celebrating the mind's power to create and to transform, Moore embodies Denise Levertov's homage to the imagination:

Our age appears to me a chaos and our environment lacks the qualities for which we could call it a culture. But by way of consolation
we have this knowledge of power that perhaps no one in such a
supposed harmonious time had; what in the greatest poets is recognizable as Imagination, that breathing of life into dust, is present in
us all embryonically—manifests itself in the life of a dream—and in
that manifestation shows us the possibility: to permeate, to quicken,
all of our life and the works we make. What joy to be reminded by
truth in dream that the Imagination does not arise from the environment but has the power to create it. [14]

This recognition of the creative power of the imagination lies at the
heart of Moore's "The Mind is an Enchanting Thing." She writes that
"the mind / feeling its way as though blind / walks along with its eyes on

the ground." In that posture, this "enchanting thing" also becomes "an enchanted thing," and Moore admits and wants to preserve both the mind's aggression and its unpredictable whimsy and susceptibility:

> It tears off the veil; tears
>   the temptation, the
> mist the heart wears,
>   from its eyes—if the heart
>   has a face; it takes apart
> dejection. It's fire in the dove-neck's
>
> iridescence; in the
>   inconsistencies
> of Scarlatti.
>   Unconfusion submits
>   its confusion to proof; it's
> not a Herod's oath that cannot change.   (CP, 134–135)

With such a combination of powers, the mind can willfully recreate an "Old Amusement Park: *Before It Became La Guardia Airport*" (CP, 210) and can rejoice at having "magnetized Bach and his family / 'to North-western,' besides five harpsichords / without which he would not leave home" (CP, 209). But even while Moore creates these and other delightful fantasies, she shows that this very enchanting and enchanted mind has limitations. In "The Mind, Intractable Thing," imagination tempts with promise but resists control. Even "with its own ax to grind, [it] sometimes / helps others." Moore asks, then, "Why can't it help me?" Instead of help, the enchanting and enchanted mind offers puzzling or even disturbing illusions: "Weren't you refracting just now / on my eye's half-closed tryptych / the image, enhanced, of a glen—." Moore is aware that such deception is possible, and her speaker goes on to ask whether the mind has, of its own accord, created the image of

>   a bird—Arizona
> caught-up-with, uncatchable cuckoo
> after two hours' pursuit, zigzagging
> road-runner, stenciled in black
> stripes all over, the tail
>   windmilling up *to defy me?* (CP, 208; italics mine)

Caught up in such troubling illusions, the speaker of the poem addresses the mind directly: "You understand terror, know how to deal / with pent-up emotion, a ballad, witchcraft. / I don't. O Zeus and O Destiny!" This speaker envies the intractability of the mind she addresses and the protection it has the potential to offer. But the imaginative control of that protective illusion eludes her:

> Unafraid of what's done,
> undeterred by apparent defeat,
> you imagnifico, unafraid
> of disparagers, death, dejection,
> have out-wiled the Mermaid of Zennor,
> > made wordcraft irresistible:
> reef, wreck, lost lad, and "sea-foundered bell"—
> as near a thing as we have to a king—
> > craft with which I don't know how to deal.   (208)

Even without absolute control, Moore knows how to deal with the recognition of limitations, and she does so in a manner as disconcerting as the realization itself. When Moore wishes to explore the discrepancy between escapist or romantic desire and the blunt inefficacy of private imaginative fictions, she employs the full range of her technique. In "A Grave," which exemplifies her practice of giving with the right hand so that she can take away with the left, Moore lulls her readers by emphasizing the beauty of the scene and then shocks them with the danger inherent in its unfathomable attraction. The poem departs from Moore's usual impersonal approach by employing direct address, but it is only generalized "Man" whom she addresses. The poem maintains the somber and foreboding tone that its first sentence establishes. The warning, ostensibly directed at the unwary addressee, soon seems to forget its concern that he is depriving others from the view he is contemplating. Instead, it evolves into an assessment of the pervasive but thus far unperceived danger:

> Man looking into the sea,
> taking the view from those who have as much right to it as you
> > have to it yourself,
> it is human nature to stand in the middle of a thing,
> but you cannot stand in the middle of this;
> the sea has nothing to give but a well excavated grave.   (CP, 49)

With that sinister warning, the poem goes on to intensify its premonition of danger by turning orderly beauty into reserve, then to repression, and finally to active but unexpected and inexplicable vengeance:

> The firs stand in a procession, each with an emerald turkey foot at
> > the top,
> reserved as their contours, saying nothing;

repression, however, is not the most obvious characteristic of the sea;
the sea is a collector, quick to return a rapacious look.   (49)

After warning that "There are others besides you who have worn that
look— / whose expression is no longer a protest; the fish no longer in-
vestigate them / for their bones have not lasted," Moore proceeds, as she
does in "The Steeple-Jack," to make the very source of danger even
more attractive. The poem admits mortal threat into this scene by reporting on the ways in which it has been overlooked but goes on to restore the image of benevolent, orderly motion. That illusion makes the
poem's ultimate deception all the more effective and unsettling.

> men lower nets, unconscious of the fact that they are desecrating a
>   grave,
> and row quickly away—the blades of the oars
> moving together like the feet of water-spiders as if there were no
>   such thing as death.
> The wrinkles progress among themselves in a phalanx—beautiful
>   under the networks of foam,
> and fade breathlessly while the sea rustles in and out of the seaweed;
> the birds swim through the air at top speed, emitting catcalls as
>   heretofore—
> the tortoise shell scourges about the feet of the cliffs, in motion
>   beneath them;   ,
> and the ocean, under the pulsation of lighthouses and the noise of
>   bell buoys,
> advances as usual, looking as if it were not that ocean in which
>   dropped things are bound to sink—
> in which if they turn and twist, it is neither with volition nor
>   consciousness.   (49–50)

This scene, especially the deception of its peaceful exterior and the apparent lack of reason in or design to its rapaciousness, reveals a side of
Marianne Moore that neither Williams nor Stevens acknowledges. It
contains the simplicity, the specificity, and the refusal to resort to "distortions or the abstract in form" (*Selected Essays,* 123) that led Williams
to claim that Marianne Moore is of all American writers the most con-
stantly a poet. It also displays the penetration beyond surface appearances that Stevens associated with a permissible escapism. But in com-
bining these qualities, in creating what clearly is the reality of her own
particulars, Moore has placed her readers in the uncomfortable position
of facing not just the insufficiency and the error of their perceptions, but
their inability—because of the scene's very attraction—to abandon hope

in it. Moreover, the danger beneath that cunning surface is so subtle and insubstantial as to be able to go on both attracting and overwhelming, both deceiving and undermining indefinitely. Occasionally this deception results in pleasant confusion, as in "Baseball and Writing" or in "Old Amusement Park." Even in "An Octopus," where one senses true danger, the result is not always stark dread, as it is in "A Grave." But Moore holds on to her ability to present that innocent engagement with deception. It is the particular reality which she occasionally and then very effectively allows to surface. Much of Moore's work is directed toward achieving this effect.

The process of dis-covering the qualities at the heart of the reality that Marianne Moore created out of her own imaginative particulars is not an easy one. The shards of Moore's work, which serve her own contemporaries as well as today's critical theorists, provide clues, but her own rhetoric remains one of absent presence. Moore shares the joyful play that William Carlos Williams brought to his American topics, but she rejects the romance with which he unconsciously treats those topics. Moore shares Stevens's attraction for escapism and, like him, recognizes the seductive lure of "the revenge of music." Nevertheless, Moore denies the possibility of escapism and writes poems that "lack" the beauty of Stevens's lines. In contrast to the transcendent analogue that Stevens's fictions proffer, Moore offers disturbing amalgamations that reject those fictions altogether. Like the essays she wrote as editor for *The Dial*, Moore's poems acknowledge the twentieth century inclusively rather than defensively. In refusing to produce either a transformed or a transcendent analogue, Moore insists upon the particulars of her own reality as a sufficient response to and a postmodern history of the twentieth century.

5 · Craftsmanship Disfigured and Restored

And tell the Maestro de pentore
That there can be no question of
His painting the walls for the monument,
As the mortar is not yet dry
And it wd. be merely work chucked away

And Kung said . . .
". . . even I can remember
A day when the historians left blanks in their writings,
I mean for things they didn't know,
But that time seems to be passing."

Ezra Pound, Cantos VIII and XIII

ALTHOUGH ONE can discern Marianne Moore's critical principles and her ideas of the imagination, both in her critical essays and at work in her poems, reading those poems can still be an experience in frustration. Like the imperious seller in "Novices" who "buys, and holds onto the money" (CP, 60), Moore remains in control of her impenetrable constructions. A master of elliptical style, she demands attention to her precise images, devotion to the syntax of her elaborate sentences, and respect for the integrity of their mysterious quotations. Moore's poems also insist upon keeping their raw mortar in view, and they do so without apology. The parts all fit in a Marianne Moore poem, but the pattern they create reverses every expectation of what a "good" modernist poem ought to be and do. Moore heaps contradiction and confusion upon one another and produces out of that amalgamation what she has called "A right good salvo of barks" (CP, 45). Marshalled into elaborate patterns, the salvo of barks presents description, observation, and snatches of colloquial speech so precise and startling that Moore tempts her readers to expect traditional poetry or at least some recognizable conclusions. Instead, her aggression predominates. Moore ends many of her poems by irrevocably undermining her readers' expectations and by presenting enigma, imbalance, and incongruity. In fact, the most consistent quality of Moore's poetry is its instability. Her images promise specificity, but they dissolve as soon as one tries to visualize them. Her epigrammatic endings fly off into abstraction instead of offering resolution that they seem to promise. Most significantly, Moore manipulates quotations in order to question the stability and even the efficacy of language.

Initially, Moore's undertaking resembles what Paul de Man calls "reading as disfiguration," [1] but Moore's disfiguration is even more radical than the one de Man attributes to Shelley. As de Man explains disfiguration, Shelley's *The Triumph of Life* warns us that nothing, "whether deed, word, thought or text, ever happens in relation, positive or negative, to anything that precedes, follows or exists elsewhere, but only as a random event whose power, like the power of death, is due to the randomness of its occurrence" (69). Then de Man admits Shelley's belief that "these events then have to be reintegrated in a historical and aesthetic system of recuperation" (69). Shelley's process thus culminates in reconstruction: "To read is to understand, to question, to know, to forget, to erase, to deface, to repeat—that is to say, the endless prosopopoeia by which all the dead are made to have a face and a voice which tells the allegory of their demise and allows us to apostrophize them in our turn" (68). Moore refuses even to suggest such a re-presentation or return. Her poems manipulate presence and absence, specificity and anonymity, with absolute control. She makes her fragments present, but she refuses to give them a face. Moore's unusual images become part of the process of her disfiguration.

Selective Vision

Many of Marianne Moore's poems center upon precise, vivid images that grow out of her synthetic constructs. Often the result is an accurate depiction of a real object, such as the image in "No Swan So Fine" of the swan itself, with "Fawn- / brown eyes," perched in its "candelabrum-tree" and wearing a "toothed-gold collar . . . to show whose bird it was" (CP, 19). In such cases the images persist and become what we have come to think of as "the raw material of poetry" (CP, 267). Sometimes, as in "People's Surroundings," this image-making results in seeing more than it is comfortable to see. Culled from a vast array of sources, the surroundings of the poem vary from the "dried bone arrangement" of "a deal table compact with the wall" to the oddity of San Antonio's "municipal bat-roost of mosquito warfare" and finally to "the acacia-like lady shivering at the touch of a hand" (CP, 55–57). The assortment becomes "dyed quicksilver let fall / to disappear like an obedient chameleon in fifty shades of mauve and amethyst." In this plethora, "where the mind of this establishment has come to the conclusion / that it would be impossible to revolve about oneself too much, / sophistication has, 'like an escalator,' 'cut the nerve of progress.'" Faced with this excess, Moore offers a solution that she employs in many poems and that gives them their characteristic instability:

> In these noncommittal, personal-impersonal expressions of
>   appearance,

the eyes knows what to skip;
the physiognomy of conduct must not reveal the skeleton;
"a setting must not have the air of being one,"
yet with X-ray-like inquisitive intensity upon it, the surfaces go back;
the interfering fringes of expression are but a stain on what stands
    out (57)

The selective vision that Moore outlines here works well enough when her constructions are openly synthetic. In other poems, however, it is unsettling. In "The Fish," for instance, Moore employs a typically intricate stanzaic pattern along with evocative, sensual language to create a scene as unfathomable as it initially seems specific. The first three sentences are clear enough. The fish "wade through [the] black jade" of a sea where "submerged shafts of the // sun . . . move themselves with spotlight swiftness" (CP, 32–33). Nevertheless, even within those sentences, Moore has hinted at the broken vision to follow. She describes the movement of one of the "crow-blue mussel-shells" with curious indirection. The movement of the sand helps a viewer to infer rather than to observe directly the broken movement of the shells. We know only that "one keeps / adjusting the ash heaps, / opening and shutting itself like // an / injured fan." The rest of the poem develops this hint of submerged movement and emphasizes its potential for violence: "The water drives a wedge / of iron through the iron edge / of the cliff" and the cliff itself shows "external / marks of abuse," both natural and deliberately inflicted. Having developed the apparent specificity of the poem to this point, Moore dissolves the scene in a flood of ambiguity. One side of the cliff provides a sheltered pool for sea life. In describing it, Moore begins a new stanza with a new sentence, a technique which, in her poems, often foretells dissolution.

All
external
    marks of abuse are present on this
    defiant edifice—
        all the physical features of

ac-
cident—lack
    of cornice, dynamite grooves, burns, and
    hatchet strokes, these things stand
        out on it; the chasm side is

dead.

Repeated
>   evidence has proved that it can live
>   on what it can not revive
>   its youth. The sea grows old in it. (32–33)

Contradiction dominates these images. "Lack of cornice," if it means a natural curve to the edge of the cliff, is certainly a physical feature of accident; but "dynamite grooves, burns, and / hatchet strokes" are just as surely not accidental. They are human interventions that "stand out" on the cliff. Thus, it should not be surprising that "the chasm side is dead." That announcement, however, makes the next two sentences entirely incomprehensible. If the chasm side is dead, ravaged as it clearly has been by the force of the water it contains, how does it *live* on the barnacles that adhere to its surface, on the shifting mussel shells that may or may not contain live mussels, and on the rest of the sliding mass of sea life that it shelters? Finally, why does the sea, clearly the most active and powerful force in this scene, grow old within this teeming shelter? Moore not only does not answer these questions, she does not even admit that she has asked them. The poem pretends that it works visually, whereas it should warn readers that images in poems are not always what they seem to be.

"Nine Nectarines" begins the process of cautioning readers when it warns against uncritically accepting surface appearances and first impressions. Moore opens the poem by criticizing the "uninquiring brush / of mercantile bookbinding," which accurately captured an arrangement of nectarines on a painted plate. The artist's portrayal of a natural scene seems accurate to a fault:

>   One perceives no flaws
>   in this emblematic group
>   of nine, with leaf window
>   unquilted by *curculio*
>   which someone once depicted on
>   this much mended plate (CP, 29)

Nevertheless, Moore adds, "It was a Chinese / who imagined this masterpiece." Thus, unlike its French and British counterparts, which depict "hunts and domestic scenes" too literally, this one succeeds because its Chinese creator "'understands / the spirit of the wilderness.'" The version of "Nine Nectarines" in *Selected Poems* admits the appeal of accurate presentation but emphasizes its shortcomings as well. Having first criticized idyllic hunt scenes depicted on the British plates, Moore tempers her reception with a pointed question:

> Yet with the gold-glossed
>   serpent handles, are there green
> cocks with 'brown beaks and cheeks
> and dark blue combs' and mammal freaks
>   that, like the Chinese Certainties
>   and sets of Precious Things
>   dare to be conspicuous?   (SP, 31)

Images must be specific and accurate. Thus, Moore concentrates on details such as the arrangement of the nectarines "by two's as peaches are, / at intervals that all may live—eight and a single one, on twigs that / grew the year before." They must also capture the mythical healing qualities of this "wild spontaneous fruit;" the precise error of the scene's unantlered moose; and the "pony appearance" of the kylin or the antelope feet of the unicorn.

In other poems, too, Moore sets up a contrast between precision without imagination and the wisdom which recognizes that the most accurate images come from portraying the wilderness of confusion. We must be "precisionists," but we must treat our subjects with "ancient punctilio / in the manner of Chinese lacquer carving, / layer after layer exposed by certainty of touch and unhurried incision / so that only so much color shall be revealed as is necessary to the picture" (CP, 59). "Critics and Connoisseurs" makes this argument explicitly. Moore admits that precise images and controlled demeanor have their appeal. She adds, though, that she likes ordinary, even misguided effort better than the safety of isolated precision. Thus she admires the charm of a

> mere childish attempt to make an imperfectly bal-
>   lasted animal stand up,
> similar determination to make a pup
>   eat his meat from a plate.   (CP, 38)

In the same poem, Moore ridicules the pristine arrogance of "a swan under the willows at Oxford, / with flamingo-colored, maple- / leaf-like feet" whose "Disbelief and conscious fastidiousness" nearly overcame its instinct for survival. She also warns that she has seen "this ambition without / understanding in a variety of forms." To illustrate her point, Moore offers a humorous example of that behavior in the parable of "fastidious ant" who, even when it "turned on / itself," failed to recognize that lack of imagination doomed its blind ambition to failure. She then concludes the poem in exasperation:

> What is
> there in being able

> to say that one has dominated the stream in an attitude of self
>> defense;
> in proving that one has had the experience
>> of carrying a stick?   (CP, 39)

Wisdom replaces blind ambition in a poem appropriately titled "The Hero." Following her inclination to deny dialectical resolution, Moore keeps both uncertainty and the desire for absolute control alive. As human as her readers, Moore's hero doesn't like "deviating head-stones / and uncertainty." Even though the hero "shrinks" from such phenomena, the images of them persist and intrude upon his consciousness "until the skin creeps." Finally, patience and curiosity become the agents that rescue the hero from his crisis. Thus, "like Pilgrim having to go slow / to find his role," today's hero must be

> tired but hopeful—
> hope not being hope
> until all ground for hope has
> vanished; and lenient, looking
> upon a fellow creature's error with the
> feelings of a mother—a
> woman or a cat.   (CP, 8–9)

Once that hero can reject the "conscious fastidiousness" of the unimaginative swan at Oxford, his vision becomes inclusive and consequently redemptive. The hero sees not an intellectual "sight" but

> the rock
> crystal thing to see—the startling El Greco
> brimming with inner light—that
> covets nothing that it has let go. This then you may know
> as the hero.   (9)

Part of the instability of Moore's images comes, thus, from her desire to insist that what seems to be clear might not be so at all. Imperfection and imaginary "fact" produce the most truthful images. In some of her later poems, Moore takes this inversion even farther. "O to Be a Dragon" avoids the question of vision altogether and privileges instead the malleability of the fables surrounding the imaginary monster of the poem. If Moore could have her way, she would be a dragon, but not primarily because the transformation would make her "a symbol of the power of Heaven." The chief pleasure, and the "Felicitous phenomenon" of Moore's fantasy would be her freedom to assume "silkworm / size" or to become "immense," and even to be "at times invisible." That same whim of fancy, should Moore come to possess it, would enable her to transform the meaningless but relentless bustle of La Guardia Airport, in which an unwary visitor might "hurry" and "worry" but would never think to "vary / the pressure till [he becomes] nearly bat blind." In Moore's transformation of this image, the commerce of the airport—its "tramcar / rattling greenish caterpillar" and the bowling-ball thunder" of the airport's corridors—would become the former amusement park's elephant who "slowly lies down aslant." Commerce would be a less pressured sort of trade:

> A businessman, the pony-paddock boy
> locks his equestrian toy—

> flags flying, fares collected,
> shooting gallery neglected—
>   half-official, half-sequestered,
>   limber-slouched against a post,
>   and tells a friend what matters least.   (CP, 210)

This imaginative recreation of forgotten leisure begins from regret. A devoted circus-goer and a regular visitor at the zoo, Moore loved any setting that offered a carnivallike atmosphere. Thus, the airport, having usurped the old amusement park's territory, evokes Moore's protest that "A predicament so dire could not / occur in this rare spot" (210). Moore escapes from the dire predicament because she privileges memory and imagination over mundane fact. The old amusement park thus magically appears:

> It's the old park in a nutshell,
> like its tame-wild carrousel—
>   the exhilarating peak
>   when the triumph is reflective
>   and confusion, retroactive.   (210–211)

In this off-handed manner, Moore triumphs over excessively literal images that do not appeal to her, and the confusion that she reactivates takes over. Its images become primary as Moore once again insists that simple vision, even when it seems to be most accurate, might need to be undermined.

Having shown that images must not depend solely on outward appearances, Moore builds upon that freedom in "The Paper Nautilus." The poem discovers the life story of the paper nautilus, but not in its commercial worth or even in its productivity. The animal constructs its beautiful shell as a shelter for its unborn progeny. The shell also serves as a gestation-period resting place for the parent paper nautilus herself—

and sometimes for her mate. The shell should not be, Moore notes as she opens the poem, "for authorities whose hopes / are shaped by mercenaries" nor the "writers entrapped by / teatime fame" (CP, 121). In proving this, the poem becomes one of Moore's most hauntingly emotional ones as she reexamines the now abandoned outward sign of the paper nautilus's plan to protect its unborn. Moore suppresses any trace of the shell's appeal to curio hunters—commercial value—and endows it instead with emotional worth. It becomes a "perishable souvenir of hope." With methodical specificity, Moore describes the now empty shell's "dull / white outside and smooth- / edged inner surface / glossy as the sea" (121). She also explains that, although the parent herself takes shelter deep within this shell—"Buried eight-fold in her own eight / arms," it does not crush the tender eggs that it guards by day and night. Once the shell's "glass ram'shorn-cradled freight" hatches, neither the parent nor the young animals need it: "The intensively / watched eggs coming from / the shell free it when they are freed" (121).

Having previously denied profit hunters and idle curiosity-seekers any claim to the paperlike shell, Moore frees herself to acknowledge more of the beauty and emotional appeal of the object. Emptied of its cargo and therefore no longer valuable for its contents or to the life it contained, the object reveals its spiritual power:

> its wasp-nest flaws
> of white on white, and close-
>
> laid Ionic chilton-folds
> like the lines in the mane of
> a Parthenon horse,
> round which the arms had
> wound themselves as if they knew love
> is the only fortress
> strong enough to trust to.   (122)

Moore invests the animal's instinctive design-making with more emotion than would be possible if one observed merely factual details. The image is also more accurate than would have been possible while the animal was engaged in the process of sustaining life. Once removed from its ordained role, the shell becomes a powerful image of its purpose. It is also paper-thin and fragile. Double vision continues.

Gordian Solutions

In the same way that Marianne Moore creates vivid images to demonstrate their fragility, she also gives to and takes away from her poems by manipulating the ways in which they end. Moore employs epigrammatic endings to undermine and to disfigure the absolute closure that those endings ordinarily suggest. From the outset, Moore's procedure becomes as problematic as she had intended it to be. Barbara Herrnstein Smith points out that in twentieth-century poetry, even "in modern poems otherwise quite dissimilar in style, one may readily observe an apparent tendency toward anti-closure."[2] Marianne Moore does not fit this pattern. She does not employ the "non-assertive conclusion" (258) that Herrnstein Smith finds in William Carlos Williams's poetry, nor are her endings the arbitrary, half-welcome interruptions employed by T. S. Eliot to extricate J. Alfred Prufrock from his "argument of insidious intent" (146). Instead, Moore's poems conclude with the sort of utterance which "seems to be the last word on its subject" (196)—the epigram. Rather than being open-ended, her poems are "hyperdetermined" in the style of epigrammatic discourse. For any epigrammatic poem, Herrnstein Smith explains, the "structural and non-structural forces of closure are so strong that expectation is not only fulfilled but exceeded" (206).

Herrnstein Smith does not discuss Moore's poetry either in her section on epigram or along with the modern poems she examines, but the first appellation fits Moore quite well. Her form is precise, and her stance is appropriately cool and imperious. Herrnstein Smith explains the approach in terms of control: "The epigrammatist is proud: He does not wish to endear or ingratiate himself to the reader. Nor is he intimate. He holds the reader at a distance, addressing him directly, but not inviting him to share experiences. (To a reader who says he does not like epigram, the epigrammatist is likely to reply, 'You are not supposed to')" (208). Moore has clearly adopted this attitude in the pronouncements that run throughout her poems. She acknowledges that her words might "indeed deprecate / offended ears" (CP, 81), and she dismisses those who cannot understand her design: "The illustration / is nothing to you without the application. / You lack half wit" (84).

Such proclamations gained Moore a reputation that at first seems to fulfill the second half of Herrnstein Smith's definition of epigrammatic poetry:

> The epigrammatist does not live in a physical world. He lives in a moral world. And although he is skeptical and toughminded, he is a moral traditionalist. The only novelty with which he surprises us is that of conventional truth. Economizing for the sake of pointedness, the epigrammatist uses short, simple sentences or clauses, and omits certain words and expressions that otherwise give to speech a tone of gracious reasonableness. The epigrammatist is not reasonable, for reason is his passion. (*Poetic Closure*, 209)

Moore fits this sobriquet except for Herrnstein Smith's remarks on the epigrammatist's passion for reason. Moore's passion is for evasion and for inversions of reason. She evades both the oversimplification that epigrammatic closure might impose on her poems and the reasonable solutions to everyday contradictions. "In the Days of Prismatic Color" exemplifies this approach by arguing that "complexity is not a crime" but that, carried "to the point of murkiness," it confuses all perceptions. "Nothing is plain" (CP, 41). The poem seems at first to follow its own advice when it laments the long-past days of dazzling but unobtruded light. That time was

> not in the days of Adam and Eve, but when Adam
>   was alone; when there was no smoke and color was
> fine, not with the refinement
>   of early civilization art, but because
> of its originality; with nothing to modify it but the
>
> mist that went up, obliqueness was a variation
>   of the perpendicular, plain to see and
> to account for   (CP, 41)

The poem goes on to explain that this sort of clarity no longer reigns: "nor did the blue-red-yellow band / of incandescence that was color keep its stripe." Once Moore makes this observation, once the pristine clarity of innocent vision has been clouded, the poem becomes, like the original unmodified scene that is its subject, "one of // those things into which much that is peculiar can be / read." And, indeed, the poem does become peculiar, even in its parts, which had at first seemed straightforward. What is the originality that predates smoke and color and "the refinement of early civilization art?" And how did light manage to be "plain to see and / to account for" if it was modified by mist? Finally, how does one distinguish between obliqueness as "a variation / of the perpendicular" and obliqueness as indirection? Moore begins to settle the matter, but she makes her solution only partial. It is a "dismal / fallacy" to believe that "insistence / is the measure of achievement and that all / truth must be dark." But the authority of that pronouncement leads to confusion rather than to light. In fact, Moore's next four sentences systematically undercut whatever certainty she had achieved:

> Principally throat, sophistication is as it al-
>
> ways has been—at the antipodes from the init-
>   ial great truths. "Part of it was crawling, part of it

> was about to crawl, the rest
>   was torpid in its lair." In the short-legged fit-
> ful advance, the gurgling and all the minutia—we have the classic
>
> multitude of feet. To what purpose!   (41–42)

Moore has used her stanzaic pattern to add yet more confusion to the poem. She ends her penultimate stanza with the word "classic." Her reader believes, at least momentarily, that Moore has promoted halting progress and disordered complexity to the status of the classic—lasting value. If that were true, it would become one of the initial great truths. Such a design would separate random particulars from the "throat" and from the strictures of sophistication. Moore's reader soon discovers, however, that the dichotomy—the antipodes between which such great truths operate—is not so clear. The gurgling and the minutiae become "the classic multitude of feet." The sentence has thus gone full circle. The short-legged fitful advance takes place; it takes place, but igno-miniously. The advance itself is circular.

Having thoroughly unsettled and confused her reader with dismal fal-lacy, Moore appears to resolve the problem. Her epigrammatic closure, however, doesn't close the poem at all. It only reinforces its circularity. In two sentences, Moore exposes the foolishness of attempting to define truth, either in terms of sophistication or as a gurgling, fitful advance:

> Truth is no Apollo
> Belvedere, no formal thing. The wave may go over it if it likes.
> Know that it will be there when it says,
>   "I shall be there when the wave has gone by."   (42)

Truth may claim that it is self-sufficient, but the stanza is incomplete. It has no fifth line, as do the others in the poem; and its second and fourth lines don't rhyme—another disfiguration of Moore's pattern. Further-more, the poem argues both sides of Moore's puzzle. Truth isn't classi-cally beautiful and powerful. Like other everyday minutiae, it can be en-gulfed on a whim. How then can one believe truth's claim that it will be there after it has been overtaken? The confusion of these unanswered questions comes not only from the paradoxical nature of the situation itself, but from the fact that Moore presents her conclusion and then un-dercuts any possibility that it works as a conclusion. The poem's ending refuses to submit to any of Barbara Herrnstein Smith's all-inclusive cate-gories for how poems end. It rejects the anticlosural style of modernist poetry, and it destroys the ironic assurance of its radical alternative—the epigram.

The apparently "unsuccessful" ending of "In the Days of Prismatic

Color" and those of other poems like it gain their power, ironically enough, because of their ability to explode into uncertainty, a state usually associated with powerlessness. Attempting to resolve the complexity of such an illusive concept as truth would be self-delusion. "When I Buy Pictures" avoids that error because its speaker adopts an air of nonchalance. She explains that personal preference and imaginative fancy, rather than rigid aesthetic principles, dictate her real and imagined purchases. Drawing the title down into the poem, Moore plunges into an uncharacteristically breezy sentence:

When I Buy Pictures

or what is closer to the truth,
when I look at that of which I may regard myself as the imaginary
    possessor,
I fix upon what would give me pleasure in my average moments
(CP, 48)

The list that follows contains items ranging from elaborate curios, such as a "medieval decorated hat-box / in which there are hounds with waists diminishing like the waist of the hour-glass, / and deer and birds and seated people," to a simple "artichoke in six varieties of blue." Moore suggests that even if the imagined possession were merely a "square of parquetry," it would probably be finely crafted. In describing another possession, she enacts one of its qualities in the line describing it. She might wish to possess "the literal biography perhaps, / in letters standing well apart upon a parchment-like expanse." The steady, unvarying rhythm of the line and the explosive percussion of its alliteration reproduce the distinctive quality of the lettering that Moore admired. Nevertheless, Moore appends to her wish list another list, one of qualification rather than of dreams. An object of which Marianne Moore might regard herself the imaginary possessor must not place too "stern an intellectual emphasis upon this quality or that," for that would "detract from one's enjoyment." Nor can the object itself be arrogant: "It must not wish to disarm anything; nor may the approved triumph easily be honored— / that which is great because something else is small." These qualifications seem merely to reinforce Moore's belief that " 'A right good salvo of barks'" (CP, 45) will suffice for poetry. But again Moore reverses her own dicta and concludes by announcing that "It comes to this: of whatever sort it is, / it must be 'lit with piercing glances into the life of things'; / it must acknowledge the spiritual forces which have made it" (48). Moore's epigrammatic pith makes the task seem easy enough until one considers what such acknowledgement might entail. The task then becomes all but impossible. What informs the piercing glance? How is the viewer to perceive those qualities? In the absence of "too stern an intellectual emphasis," can an artist be at all sure of acknowledging those spiritual forces? By refusing to be more specific about what satisfied her taste, Moore presents, in spite of having warned against it, her own "satire upon curiosity in which no more is discernible / than the intensity of the mood." The task has become a conundrum.

The history of the poem complicates the puzzle further, since Moore altered the poem's original epigrammatic ending. When the poem first appeared in the July 1927 issue of *The Dial*, Moore had employed an ending purporting to show how one can acknowledge those spiritual forces. The poem explains that the object must be "lit with piercing glances into the life of things," but it presents the last three lines in a different order and concludes with yet another line. In the *Dial* version, the poem closes with these four lines:

> It comes to this: of whatever sort it is,
> it must acknowledge the forces which have made it;
> it must be "lit with piercing glances into the life of things;"
> then I "take it in hand as a savage would take a looking-glass."
>
> (71, July 1921, 33)

While certainly not "too stern" in its "intellectual emphasis," this concluding line is hopelessly ambiguous. How does a savage take a looking-glass in hand? Fearfully, in order to deflect the blinding light it might find unsettling? Narcissus-like in self-enchanted fantasy? As a tool for self-revelation or for outward exploration? In any case, the task is impossible, and Moore reinforces the deadlock of her challenge. She can end the poem cleverly, but she leaves her reader confused. The closing lines of the second version are less coy but no less enigmatic. When Moore discards the mirror of her first version and takes up the pen instead, the "forces" that a work must acknowledge become "spiritual" ones, and thus even more intangible.

The poem has progressed through three stages. It opens with its speaker leisurely browsing among objects that she might wish to own. It then moves to a closer inspection of those objects and produces a list of such variety that the sole unifying characteristic of its objects seems to be that they caught the imaginary possessor's attention and fancy. Finally, the poem discards pleasure as a goal and replaces it with rules. This change in tone reverberates in the closing lines, particularly in the poem's revised form. The poem began when the prospective buyer "fix[ed] upon what would give [her] pleasure in [her] average moments." That ability to give pleasure must somehow have inspired the making of the object in the first place. Not content to let the challenge be resolved so easily, Moore surreptitiously erases the role of pleasure. She warns against too much "intellectual emphasis," but introduces and foregrounds it herself. She calls for "piercing glances into the life of things" and insists that one discover and acknowledge "spiritual forces." The enigma gains power because Moore's epigrammatic style makes the task sound so simple. Her conclusion rejects idle speculation and pretends to offer a straightforward evaluation. Instead, as in so many other instances of Moore's epigrammatic closure, the poem opens rather than constrains experience.

Moore's disfiguration of epigrammatic closure in these two poems reveals her disfiguration of the form. "In the Days of Prismatic Color" argues that neither Apollonian stability and truth nor complexity compounded into alleged sophistication will offer a productive point of focus. "When I Buy Pictures" refuses to privilege either unfiltered emotional preference or purely intellectual goals. The poem thus returns the burden of defining value to the creators themselves. Each poem creates a vivifying deadlock by employing and then denying the hyperdetermined effect of epigrammatic form. The practice runs throughout Moore's poems, but she addresses it specifically in "Charity Overcoming Envy," which recounts a tale depicted in a fifteenth-century tapestry. Charity, riding on an elephant, meets Envy, riding on a dog. Envy cries to charity for rescue from the fate that he imagines must be due him. The elephant, an agent of stability in "Melancthon," plays the same role here. He convinces the victim "that Destiny is not devising a plot." Moore concludes the poem with one of her most impenetrable epigrams. It declines to explain the outcome of the encounter, but it does at least offer a suggestion for reading this poem and others like it:

> The problem is mastered—insupportably
> tiring when it was impending.
> Deliverance accounts for what sounds like an axiom.
>
> The Gordian knot need not be cut.   (CP, 216)

The Ethics of Borrowing

When Moore weaves so obtrusive a knot and then insists that it need not be cut, she pushes her reader to the limits of logical tolerance. She tells us to hold on to our old methods of reading and also to discard them. We should defend old ideas and relinquish them. Moore is equally aggressive and unabashedly subversive when she turns her disfiguration of language upon quotations. On one level, Moore undermines her readers' expectations, but more significantly she undermines the spoken word itself. Just as Moore continually creates and promotes instability by manipulating images and by denying the expectations established by her epigrams, she disfigures both her own sentences and the sources from which she borrowed their words. The process begins innocently enough with quotation marks. Moore marks the words as borrowed but also claims them as her own. Quotation marks litter her poems; and as their traditional role dictates, they say two things at once. These marked words are *less* important than others on this page because they have a more distant origin. These words are *more* important than the others on the page and have been set off in order to make that difference evident and permanent. Like the scrupulous critic in "When I Buy Pictures," the writer who carefully documents her poaching does not want to triumph easily by making her sources small—or in this case invisible. But the borrower occasionally seems overly generous, since the quotation marks disturb the reader's sense of the sentence. In "Marriage," for instance, it is often clear what "he" and "she" are saying about the institution and about one another; but it is not so easy to determine who "he" and "she" are. One cannot identify the "he" who thought that Diana " 'darkeneth her countenance / as a bear doth,'" or the one who observed that " 'Married people often look that way'" (CP, 66). Certainly Moore's reader will want to identify the "he" who believes that

> "for love that will
> gaze an eagle blind,
> that is with Hercules
> climbing the trees
> in the garden of the Hesperides,
> from forty-five to seventy
> is the best age,"   (66)

And most readers will want to know whether that "he" is the same one who thought that in the fight to be affectionate " 'no truth can be fully known / until it has been tried / by the tooth of disputation'" (66).

Moore, however, never intended to answer these questions. She had achieved part of her task simply by marking the words as quotations. Not content with that initial disfiguration, Moore goes on to put the markings themselves under erasure. In doing so she refuses either to erase the words entirely or to claim them fully as her own. Only when Moore wants to use her borrowed phrases to represent actual discourse does the syntax of her sentence even acknowledge that the marks are there. In "An Octopus," Moore describes the way in which "fir-trees, in 'the magnitude of their root systems,' / rise aloof from these maneuvers 'creepy to behold'" (CP, 71). She does not, however, suggest that this voice within the text represents direct discourse. The same is true for Moore's description of the poem's glacier itself; but there is another complication:

"Picking periwinkles from the cracks"
or killing prey with the concentric rigor of the python,
it hovers forward "spider fashion
on its arms" misleadingly like lace   (71)

This passage is another example of Moore's use of quotation marks in the absence of any of their more common functions, and the syntax of the sentence absolutely denies any grammatical function for the markings. Moreoever, the sentence's two most original observations remain unmarked. Moore claims those analogies—of the octopus as a rapacious python and as a swatch of misleading lace—for herself. But she both claims *and* disavows the rest of the sentence. Moore declares war on the perfect phrases that she borrows, but she prefers the war itself to victory. The sentences remain as unsolved conundrums, just as they do when Moore pillages the domain of epigram. The outcome is deliberately ironic. Moore generates meaning by suppressing it, as the notes to her poems dutifully acknowledge.

In the four lines quoted above, for instance, the periwinkle passage came from a *London Graphic* story published in August 1923; and the spider fashion phrase, from the *Illustrated London News* for June 28, 1924. Since the first note explains that "quoted lines of which the source is not given are from the Department of Interior Rules and Regulations, *The National Parks Portfolio* (1922)," one naturally wonders whether the British sources deal specifically with the poem's subject, Mount Tacoma's glacier. Moore's other sources for "An Octopus" are Ruskin, Cardinal Newman, a philosophy textbook, an American travel guide, and a phrase "overheard at the circus." The suppressed information thus reifies the confusing deception that the poem seeks to enact.

In other notes, Moore gives away more information than she does about the sources for her words in "An Octopus," but she invariably disfigures these sources. At times, Moore suppresses a quotation's referential meaning and disavows its content. Elsewhere she tampers with the words themselves. When Moore openly disfigures a quotation's referential meaning, her admission is part of the poem's design. The suppressed version of "Poetry"—an all-encompassing example of Moore's process of disfiguration that I shall explore later in this chapter—claims that "till the poets among us can be 'literalists of the imagination,'" we shall not have poetry. But Moore's notes seem to throw even that assertion into question. Her source was *Ideas of Good and Evil*, a 1903 study of Yeats by A. H. Bullen. The exact quotation, as the notes reproduce it, reveals the extent of Moore's plunder:

p. 182 "The limitation of his view was from the very intensity of his vision; he was too literal a realist of the imagination, as others are of

> nature; and because he believed that the figures seen by the mind's
> eye, when exalted by inspiration, were 'eternal existences,' symbols
> of divine essences, he hated every grace of style that might obscure
> their lineaments." (CP, 267–268)

Moore seems to have included the sentence in its entirely in order to
share with her readers the joke of altering and yet retaining a source, a
quotation. The passage itself is typical of many that Moore included in
her reading diaries. There, as here, she merely copied an item without
adding any comment of her own. But if the note itself doesn't make
Moore's comment clear, the way in which she manipulates the quotation
certainly does. The original phrase is "too literal a realist of the imagination." Moore has also suppressed Bullen's meaning. Rather than dismiss-
ing Yeats entirely for his devotion to fancy, Moore makes his "excess" the
absolute criterion for writing good poetry. Those who achieve that level
will be "above / insolence and triviality" and will be able to present
"'imaginary gardens with real toads in them'" (CP, 267).

Moore has mastered the skill of appropriating, which she had praised
in her early essay on Samuel Butler. But she is less gracious when it
comes to acknowledging and respecting the integrity of the words she
borrows. In "Novices," Moore scrambles her sources methodically. She
suppresses their individual rhythm and dissolves the context from which
she removed them so that the words carry no referential meaning at all.
The poem begins by announcing that "novices / anatomize their work"
(CP, 60). Those novices are vain and foolish purveyors of art, and when
Moore anatomizes their behavior, she finds that they have no confidence
in their own judgment:

> the little assumptions of the scared ego confusing the issue
> so that they do not know "whether it is the buyer or the seller
>   who gives the money"—
> an abstruse idea plain to none but the artist,
> the only seller who buys, and holds onto the money.   (60)

Moore invites us to anatomize her poem and shows us that she has
bought and held onto a quotation from Anatole France—"Is it the buyer
or the seller who gives the money?" (CP, 270). She also scrupulously
shows that she has altered this quotation and another that appears a few
lines later. Foolish critics fancy themselves wise and "present themselves
as a contrast to sea-serpented regions 'unlit by the half-lights of a more
conscious art'" (CP, 60). The source was A. R. Gordon's *The Poets of the
Old Testament*, a subject of great interest to Moore. Gordon's comment
was that Hebrew poetry is "lit by half lights of a more conscious art" (CP,

270). It is neither the wording nor context alone that Moore altered, but the purpose of the words and their integrity. Pompous critics can present themselves in whatever way they choose, but Moore calls them " 'Dracontrine cockatrices, perfect and poisonous.' " She doesn't insist that the critics themselves actually used those words, but she makes it a distinct possibility.

Here and in other poems, Moore keeps the voices within her text at an inchoate level. She suggests that foreign voices *might* be present in the text, but she does not push her claim. That uncertainty in itself reinforces the degree of Moore's disfiguration. She claims and controls the lines as fully as she needs to, but she never lets them interfere with the syntax of her sentences. Nowhere is this more pervasive and active than in "Baseball and Writing," a poem "Suggested by post-game broadcasts" (CP, 211). As fractured and excited as the broadcasts that inspired it, the poem shows by its brilliant arrangement of fragments of language— none of them identified except within the poem itself—that "writing is exciting / and baseball is like writing" (CP, 221). Unlike the subdued quotations of other poems, the ones here take over the text. More than anything else that Moore has published, this poem captures her whimsical side, particularly in the third stanza, and it also captures the exciting possibilities of language and of writing. The precise and obvious rhyme scheme reinforces Moore's playful tone, and the broken language suggests that far more of the stanza than its few marked phrases is appropriated quotation:

> When three players on a side play three positions
> and modify conditions,
> > the massive run need not be everything.
> > > "Going, going . . ." Is
> > > it? Roger Maris
> > has it, running fast. You will
> > never see a finer catch. Well . . .
> > "Mickey, leaping like the devil"—why
> > > gild it, although deer sounds better—
> snares what was speeding toward its treetop nest,
> > one-handing the souvenir-to-be
> > meant to be caught by you or me.   (CP, 221–222)

The number of emotional turns and returns that Moore accomplishes here is astounding, and the power with which she invests language is even more remarkable. She conflates scenes, stops time, and creates first excitement and then hope, only to snatch it all away. Her message is two-sided. Language can create whatever it wants to; but it is, after all, only an imagined creation. The poem captures both the power of language and the fragility of speech.

"Light is Speech" also explores that power of language, but in a contemplative rather than a celebratory mood. "Light is Speech" takes its words and its inspiration from a history of lighthouses, an historical account by Voltaire, and a quotation from Montaigne. Moore acknowledges and also erases these sources, but she puts the Statue of Liberty at the center of the poem. French in its origin and representative of the freedom which the United States can offer, the statue embodies the poem's theme—that speech is light and that light is speech. Speech is words; and when those words are Voltaire's or Montaigne's, they speak freedom. Voltaire was unable to stop the execution of Jean Calas, who had been unjustly accused of murdering his son. Nevertheless, as Moore's notes report—in Voltaire's own words, Voltaire *"fut le premier qui s'éleva en sa favor"* (CP, 277). Montaigne, who was unexpectedly released after having been captured by bandits, explained: "I was told that I owed my deliverance to my bearing and the uncowed resoluteness of my speech, which showed that I was too good a fellow to hold up" (277). For Moore, even a lighthouse such as "the Creach'h / d'Ouessant light- / house on its defenseless dot of / rock, is the descendant of Voltaire // . . . of unarmed / Montaigne" (CP, 97). The image of light and speech as cooperative powers run throughout the poem, and Moore wants speech to perform the function of all types of light:

> One can say more of sunlight
>   than of speech; but speech
>   and light, each
> aiding each—when French—
> have not disgraced that still
> unextirpated adjective.
> Yes, light is speech. Free frank
> impartial sunlight, moonlight,
> starlight, lighthouse light,
>   are language.   (97)

The language of light is freedom, entry, and knowledge; and speech has the power to enact freedom. "The word France," Moore explains, "means / enfranchisement; means one who can / 'animate whoever thinks of her'" (98). The examples of light as speech and speech as light are inspiring, but they have limitations as well. Voltaire's impassioned plea came too late and was thus only symbolic. Montaigne's was even more limited. He was a persuasive rhetorician, but his rhetoric showed only that that he was a hearty fellow. Lighthouses, especially the chiefly symbolic Statue of Liberty, speak welcome, safety, and even freedom; but they do so while poised, like the Creach'h d'Ouessant, on a "defenseless dot of / rock" (97).

"Light is Speech" also argues, then, that language leads to no end. Defenseless and almost totally hermetic, it becomes animated only when someone thinks of it. Moore has laid bare the skeleton of disfigured language. Neither words themselves nor their referential meanings are stable. Words joined together have referential meaning, but it is fragile and tentative. They can be withdrawn or interrupted at the slightest whim. Yet Moore by no means capitulates into silence. Her quotations *are* disfigured, but they speak. They repeat instability but also show that language has become a " 'precipitate of dazzling impressions'" (CP, 61). Throughout Moore's disfiguration, the components of language retain their raw power. "The spontaneous unforced passion of the Hebrew language" grew out of words, " 'an abyss of verbs full of reverberations and tempestuous energy'" (CP, 61). As this line and so many others show, the perfect phrase withstands disfiguration. Moore's quotations thus become the ultimate disfiguration—tropes for the primacy of written words and the fragility of speech. The quotations interrupt and comment upon discourse, but the discourse they interrupt is Moore's own. Ironically, then, Moore restores what she has just disfigured. Discourse is fragile, but it can continue.

In "Poetry," the components of Moore's disfiguration—distortion, suppression, and restoration—converge. She tampered with the poem incessantly, shortening some of its stanzas and even the basic pattern of the poem itself. She omitted it from her collection in *A Marianne Moore Reader* but relented partially in *Complete Poems,* where it becomes merely a three-line shadow of its former selves. Not content with simple distortion and suppression, Moore then restored the poem by including the "longer" version in her notes. Moore had explained in "A Note on the Notes" that she had "not yet been able to outgrow" her "hybrid method of composition," but another of her comments seems closer to the truth. It refers to her work as "the donkey that finally found itself being carried by its masters" (CP, 262). That turnabout becomes complete in Moore's ultimate disfiguration—her effacement and restoration of the very poem that anthologists most like to borrow. The poem exemplifies the precise but fragile images that are forever receding from her poems, and it employs parabasis to allow some of her favorite writers to have their own say about poetry. Moore's alternate epigrammatic endings serve to compound the matter. The three-line version of "Poetry" calls poetry "a place for the genuine" (CP, 36), and the conclusion of the "longer version" elaborates upon that without becoming more specific:

> if you demand on the one hand,
> the raw material of poetry in
>   all its rawness and
>   that which is on the other hand
>   genuine, you are interested in poetry.   (CP, 267)

Although we are interested, we might also be puzzled, and Moore wants it to stay that way. The version of "Poetry" that appeared in the second edition of *Observations* and that has been suppressed so successfully that even some of Moore's bibliographers miss it concludes with what seems to be a reprimand: "We do not admire what we cannot understand; / enigmas are not poetry."[3] Yet Moore perversely insists that her poems remain enigmatic. By restoring what she has disfigured and effaced and by declaring war on the perfect phrase, Moore insists that we accept her radical view of language. In it, words gain power by being removed or, as she would put it, rescued from ownership, history, and meaning; but the discourse to which they contribute raw material remains unstable and unresolved. Moore has, as William Carlos Williams put it, wiped soiled words clean. She has replaced traditional notions of discourse with "a right good salvo of barks."

6 ▪ "And You Have Smiled"

And we have heard the fauns chiding Proteus
in the smell of hay under the olive trees.
And the frogs singing against the fauns in the half light

And . . .   Ezra Pound, Canto II

IN THE SEARCH for "a method of conclusions" Moore presents a critical
problem that goes beyond the recognition of her disfiguration of language. Clearing away the biographical and interpretive myths that have
surrounded the poet and recognizing that her editorship was an altogether witty undertaking show merely what she was not. Moore's self-
acknowledged method of composition methodically denies chronological boundaries, but it does not immediately suggest an identity of its
own. Instead, Moore so skillfully quotes and enacts her sources that her
prose style seems to change according to its subject. Her work becomes a
Rorschach test for readers, so much so that even the most sympathetic
among them miss the radical implications of her work. Moore insists
nevertheless that she can control the images and words that she manipulates; she also insists that her control does not make those words stable.
In some cases, this leads to a critical impasse which Moore herself predicted: "We do not admire what we cannot understand." [1]

Moore's refusal to submit to traditional methods of interpretation continues to be a stumbling block, not only for such exclusively male do-
mains as New Criticism but for Moore's critics who are female and even
feminists as well. In an essay entitled "Feminist Criticism in the Wilderness," Elaine Showalter has identified the challenge facing contemporary feminist critics by comparing it to the one Geoffrey Hartman
outlined in *Criticism in the Wilderness*. While Showalter points out that
"feminist critics may be startled to find [themselves] in this band of theoretical pioneers, since in the American literary tradition the wilderness
has been an exclusively male domain," [2] she also recognizes that the
challenge of open-minded reading goes beyond gender stereotypes. One
must, she believes, fashion an effective methodology out of the "wilderness of theory" that lies behind feminist ideology or out of that impossible state, resolute disinterestedness. Neither extreme proves helpful
in approaching Marianne Moore. Showalter points to one potential
stumbling block when she explains that openly feminist theory "makes
itself defiantly vulnerable [and thus] virtually bares its throat to the

knife, since our professional taboos against self-revelation are so strong" (189). Showalter rightly believes, however, that critics must take such defiant paths: "The tight-lipped Olympian intelligence of such texts as Elizabeth Hardwick's *Seduction and Betrayal* or Susan Sontag's *Illness as a Metaphor* can seem arid and strained" (189).

While Olympian approaches, like predetermined New Critical studies, miss Marianne Moore's ironic wordplay, polemical feminist critics, more often than not, merely lament the absence of confessional material. Barbara Herrnstein Smith offers an alternative approach that moves away from traditional interpretation and therefore never does become lost in the wilderness between the two extremes that Showalter identifies. Like the speaker in Moore's poem "New York," who "stand[s] outside and laugh[s] since to go in is to be lost," Smith begins "on the margins of discourse." That beginning permits a reader "to recognize a poem as a fictive rather than a natural discourse, as a verbal artwork rather than an event in Nature." This method thus "acknowledges [the poem] as the product of a human design in accord with certain valued human effects."[3] Smith adds that recognizing a poet's fictions as such keeps a reader aware of the poet who is writing those words and thereby creating that fiction. Like Nietzsche, then, commentators on poetry can recognize that "consciousness does not really belong to the existence of man as an individual but rather to that in him which is community or herd."[4] Nietzsche goes on to explain that while "the familiar is that to which we are accustomed . . . that to which we are accustomed is hardest to 'know'; that is to see as a problem, that is to see as strange, as abstract, as 'outside us' . . ." (68).

Thus, by defining the "margins of discourse" and identifying the poetic fiction that lies within it, a critic can begin to focus on the work itself and in a poet's own terms. Herrnstein Smith's approach is in this way compatible with Showalter's plea for a return to "the close and extensive knowledge of women's texts" for which "no theory, however suggestive, can be a substitute." Showalter argues that we must develop an eclectic approach "to what women actually write, not . . to a theoretical, political, metaphoric, or visionary ideal of what women ought to write" (205).

An ideal vision of "what women ought to write" has affected recent feminist as well as formalist studies of Marianne Moore, and treating her poetry as fictive discourse eliminates that tendency. Moore herself gives her readers clues that her work is a fictive discourse, and following those clues keeps Moore the person in view and brings together the poetic strategies that this study has been exploring. Moore's poetry emerges as a one-sided conversation that questions and reverses the literary tradition of which she was a part. Her poetry is a calculated speech act that refuses to give absolute priority either to speech or to the texts that replace speech. Words, quotations, images, and fragments retain their own integrity, but the design of the poem which they compose is equally forceful. Like the chintz china swan perched on but not taken over by the Louis XVI candelabra and still able to evoke the swart blind look and gondoliering legs of its model, Moore's poems achieve their identity and integrity by being deceptively elusive and unfathomable.

Ironic Deflection

One must approach Moore's fictive discourse by examining both Moore's own clues about the demanding creative design of her work and the ways in which contemporary feminist and formalist critics have missed or misinterpreted that design. As though in conscious battle, the lines are clearly drawn. On the one side, Moore predicts, without regret, that we might neither admire nor understand her poetry. In response, Moore's critics scramble for methods of interpretation. She refuses to budge, and her critics cannot abandon their interpretive impulse. Having predicted the unfavorable response to her work as early as 1919 in the first version of "Poetry," Moore would certainly have answered her critics by explaining in the true spirit of the avant-garde, "You are not supposed to like it."

Occasionally Moore seems to revel in dislike and misunderstanding. In "The Monkey Puzzle," for instance, she insists that her work remain

a true curio in this bypath of curio-collecting,
it is worth its weight in gold, but no one takes it
from these woods in which society's not knowing is colossal,
the lion's ferocious chrysanthemum head seeming kind by
    comparison.
This porcupine-quilled, complicated starkness—
this is beauty—"a certain proportion in the skeleton which gives the
    best results."
One is at a loss, however, to know why it should be here
in this morose part of the earth—
to account for its origin at all;
but we prove, we do not explain our birth.   (CP, 80)

Moore's message is as severe as it is clear. The loss is on the part of those who do not understand. The stark but dangerous, beautiful but unfathomable curio gains power from knowing that it need not explain itself. For the critic, such nonchalance is a problem. We know, all too often, that we do not understand; yet we cannot not like what intrigues us so much. Even approaching the poetry soon threatens to become one of "The Labors of Hercules." One hardly wants to be caught trying to "popularize the mule" or "to persuade one of austere taste, proud in the possession of a home, and a musician— / that the piano is a free field for etching; that his 'charming tadpole notes' / belong to the past when one had the time to play them" (CP, 53). These lines argue for abandoning mindless allegiance to the past, a Herculean labor by any standard. But Moore insists upon her right to create a poetry that breaks rules. She tries thus

> to persuade those self-wrought Midases of brains
> whose fourteen-carat ignorance aspires to rise in value, augurs
>   disappointment,
> that one must not borrow a long white beard and tie it on
> and threaten with the scythe of time the casually curious   (53)

The product of such daring and irreverent rule-breaking will be powerful indeed. In fact, Moore's rule-breaking gains much of its power by confounding those who have not previously encountered such invasive and evasive tactics. Breaking rules will "teach the bard with too elastic a selectiveness / that one detects creative power by its capacity to conquer one's detachment" (53). Once detected, such creative power turns out to

>   have more elasticity than logic;
> it flies along in a straight line like electricity,
> depopulating areas that boast of their remoteness   (53)

Creative power, then, comes in surprising forms. While efficient, it might not be logical; and its operations are surely capricious.

In "Four Quartz Crystal Clocks" Moore develops this theme further and offers additional clues about the nature of her fictive discourse. The poem superimposes examples of accuracy, either achieved or missed, upon the related attempts to control accuracy. The opening of the poem sets the stage for the variety of its layers and consists of Moore's pronouncement that accuracy is simply a matter of relativity. Moore begins with examples of precision but quickly introduces concomitant isolation and contradiction:

> There are four vibrators, the world's exactest clocks;
>   and these quartz time-pieces that tell
> time intervals to other clocks,
>   these worksless clocks work well   (CP, 115)

In order to maintain their accuracy, these "quartz time-pieces" must be "kept in / the 41° Bell / Laboratory time // vault." Ironically, they "work well" and keep time "independently the same" because they are "worksless." The clocks also "punctualize" some of our typical " 'instruments of truth' "—the radio, the cinema, and the press. One cannot, however, be certain that those instruments will disseminate information accurately. In an extreme example, "certain Arabs have not heard—that Napoleon / is dead. . ." Even within the protective isolation of its time vault, the worksless timepiece is vulnerable. We learn, for instance,

> that a quartz prism when
> the temperature changes, feels
> the change and that the then
> electrified alternate edges
> oppositely charged, threaten
> careful timing; so that

> this water-clear crystal as the Greeks used to say,
> this "clear ice" must be kept at the
> same coolness.   (115)

It inevitably follows that the accuracy which needs to be so carefully guarded can hardly be maintained outside its already vulnerable environment. The scientist knows that repetition "should be / synonymous with accuracy." Scientific observation, therefore, seems trustworthy enough to ensure that the "lemur-student can see / that an aye-aye is not // an angwan-tíbo, potto, or loris." Beyond such esoterica, however, accuracy vanishes, particularly in the realm of language. A seaside visitor "should not" confuse the hotel's "bell-boy" with the "buoy-ball," but the poem shows that this is not only possible but likely. Thus one is hardly persuaded by Moore's further denial of inaccuracy—"nor could a / practiced ear confuse the glass / eyes for taxidermists // with eye-glasses from the optometrist."

Having set the stage for amusing misperceptions, Moore concludes "Four Quartz Crystal Clocks" with an intricately layered puzzle. Dialing the Bell Telephone number for the time will elicit from that familiar household machine not simply information but the opportunity for a nearly Derridean instance of repetition and difference:

> And as
> Meridian-7 one-two
> one-two gives, each fifteenth second
> in the same voice, the new
> data—"The time will be" so and so—
> you realize that "when you
> hear the signal," you'll be

hearing Jupiter or jour pater, the day god—
   the salvaged son of Father Time—
telling the cannibal Chronus
   (eater of his proxime
newborn progeny) that punctuality
   is not a crime.   (116)

Moore has adopted but altered the Jupiter-Chronus myth to suit her own purpose. True to the myth, Chronus plans to devour his children, and true to the myth Rhea saves her child by deceiving the cannibal. But this salvaged son is the very one whose voice we hear portioning out time, the realm of his conquered father. He also becomes, in Moore's continued punning, "the day god." He escapes, thus, from the dark chaos which, myth tells us, produced Chronus. Jupiter also continues the work of his father. The day god salvages whatever suits him from the past and dismisses the rest of his heritage. Chaos produced both heaven and hell, and those in turn produced Chronus. Chronus's progeny, Jupiter, becomes a conquerer, one who wills himself to be a day god whose power controls not only measured time but daylight, vision in its broadest sense. This day vision mitigates but cannot entirely triumph over total chaos, the state that Edith Hamilton calls "formless confusion . . . brooded over by unbroken darkness."[5] Out of light comes repetition, which does not achieve but must pass for scientific accuracy. Ironically, then, this conquerer's best skill repeats that of his father's domain. Portioning out time, the salvaged son of Father Time is his own best representative. The "day-god" concludes that "punctuality / is not a crime." Falling short of accuracy, he could hardly be punctual, but he escapes time altogether and becomes the supreme ruler of heaven and earth.

The punning and disconnected but startlingly appropriate allusions of "Four Quartz Crystal Clocks" appear throughout Moore's poetry and make her, in the eyes of some recent feminist readers, a product of the Olympian intelligence that Elaine Showalter finds in Susan Sontag and Elizabeth Hardwick. This charge deserves careful examination since only Olympian and thoroughly unpolemical studies seem to avoid judging Moore on terms that are not her own. Feminist criticism claims that Moore is a poet trapped in a role defined and circumscribed by her identity as a women. She does not, therefore, fulfill her readers' expectations of what women poets "ought to write." Suzanne Juhasz's perceptive study of American women's poetry, *Naked and Fiery Forms,* and Bonnie Costello's academic rather than feminist treatment of Moore in *Imaginary Possessions* represent the contrasting forms in which this perception has been expressed. Each breaks new ground for Moore criticism but ultimately judges the poet on the grounds that have been previously established by male commentators. On the other hand, Helen Vendler and Laurence Stapleton avoid the language of these studies and treat Moore's personality unpolemically. In doing so, however, they miss the implications of Moore's fictive discourse. A review of these four works shows how Moore's critics have recognized but not fully understood her clues to her disguise.

Juhasz begins her study of the women's tradition in modern American poetry with Dickinson and concludes it with Adrienne Rich. She devotes a full chapter to Marianne Moore, but finds the poetry "severely limited." Moore's work is "necessary in order that the women's tradition might develop within the legitimacy of the masculine tradition; but it is characterized, as much by denial as by affirmation, by defense more often than attack." [6] Moore's stature is limited because her poetic achievement is limited. It does not, like "the great works of Eliot, Pound, Williams, and Stevens, transcend the original confinements of the Imagist aesthetic and rely heavily on personal experience . . . as translated into universal truths and generalities" (35). Moore's belief in chastity " 'as a universally regarded asset' " contributed, Juhasz believes, to Moore's achievement. But Juhasz faces that recognition with evident ambivalence:

> She was so successful in the literary world because she could at once capitalize on and repress different aspects of her femininity. Her feminine virtues of "deference" and "modesty" and charm were the ones with which men are most comfortable (and flattered); while in opting for nonsexuality, she escaped those feminine characteristics that threaten, especially in a woman who also claims—through intelligence and talent—to be an equal. She did not compete as a woman, although she may have charmed as one. When she writes about the "particular strength" that chastity confers, she writes from direct experience. Chastity is non-engagement; it leaves one in a position of safety. Like so many of the animals upon whom she focused her poetic vision, she adapted to her environment and the problems it posed with a skill that may have been unconscious but was nonetheless profitable. (39)

The profit, according to Juhasz, is a limited one. In defining Moore's contribution to the tradition of women's poetry, Juhasz offers perceptive and sympathetic readings of individual poems, but she concludes her treatment of Moore where it began. Moore's attempt "to get into the tradition" led to her "marked exclusion of feminine experience from art. 'Woman' and 'poet' were separated as the most effective means of achieving professional success" (35). While Juhasz casts this opening remark in the passive voice, the agent of that separation, in Juhasz's eyes, was Moore herself. The concluding paragraph of the chapter employs active voice and further modifies Moore's success: "Marianne Moore did not exaggerate her sense of danger. In her life and in her art, she trod delicately, purposefully, skillfully through enemy lines, deflecting attack by eluding it, by denying it, by never appearing to be at battle and thus gaining a victory that may have been qualified by the very methods used to gain it but which was nevertheless a prize that few before her had won" (54). These comments indicate Juhasz's profound discomfort as she attempts to come to terms with the unfortunate compromises Moore chose to make—unfortunate, that is, in Juhasz's eyes. I repeat them not to belittle Juhasz's effort but to show that her work has begun the critical task of defining Moore's accomplishment, of showing us how to read, read with fresh eyes "that to which we are accustomed."

From this beginning, feminist studies can continue along the lines Elaine Showalter suggests when she defends the importance of identifying specifically feminist critical concerns: "The point is that as long as we operate within the global geography of the Great Tradition, we will learn nothing new about women's writing; we will be gradually led to subordinate, summarize, and forget it. Our ideas about the important women's texts will be based on a handful of certified Great Books."[7] Nevertheless, Showalter adds, "feminist criticism cannot define women's writing solely as the expression of the victimized, the suffering, and the misunderstood" (164). This is particularly true if one believes, as many readers do, that Marianne Moore's victimization and suffering grew out of her willful self-abnegation and that today's critical misunderstanding follows from what Juhasz calls Moore's misguided effort "to play by the boys' rules" (4). Although Juhasz must be admired for her honesty in identifying and evaluating what she sees as Moore's limited achievement, I do not believe that Moore's poetry reflects accommodations to "the 'double bind' of the woman artist.'" Moore knew that she would have "to state her self definitions in code form, disguising passion as piety, rebellion as obedience."[8] The task is to see the code, as Moore made sure was possible, and to see then what Moore said within the terms of that code.

Bonnie Costello's *Imaginary Possessions* is as academic and unpolemical as Juhasz's book is openly feminist, but the two critics address many of the same questions. Whereas Juhasz sees Moore accommodating her private needs to the demands of a largely male circle of poets and critics, Costello finds defensiveness when she explores "some of the ways Moore places a poem's various orders in a dynamic relation."[9] For instance, Costello's treatment of Moore's complex method of "plain speaking" rightly claims that Moore "involves her readers creatively in the process of interpreting experience." Costello insists, nevertheless, that "Moore never felt entirely at ease with her prosodic practice." Instead, she calls Moore's technique "a mark of the poet's reticence . . . of humility" (185). Costello's analysis of this technique removes any hint of passion and rebellion from Moore's creativity: "For Moore a poem is *not* a functional utterance, rather it is an ordering of language. The poet's function is not to say something, so much as to creatively order and reimagine our sayings" (185). The poems deserve praise and admiration, but they remain only Moore's "inevitable linguistic mediation of experience" (182).

Imaginary Possessions seems at first to represent the formalist end of the continuum that Showalter outlines—feminist ideology at the one extreme and resolute disinterestedness at the other. But Costello's formalism, as much as any polemical approach, mingles comments about what Moore actually writes with ideas about what she ought to have written: "Moore's greatest poetry does not deal with the major myths of our culture, with tragic or epic themes" (13). Costello rightly claims that "we learn little about Moore's poetry by imposing on it preconceived notions of the American artist," but she goes on, nevertheless, to judge the poetry in terms of New Critical standards for good American poetry: "The native, the genuine, the vernacular in Moore, is well schooled in urbanity and restraint" (246). Costello thus admires the temperament that Juhasz regrets, but each evaluation judges Moore according to preconceived ideas about what she ought to have written.

Laurence Stapleton and Helen Vendler avoid this error by ignoring the qualities that trouble and mislead Juhasz and Costello. Like Costello, Stapleton recognizes Moore's persistent mediation of experience, but she sees that wordplay as evidence of "the poet's advance" and as a method of saying a great deal. She claims, thus, that while Moore's later poems may "divert the reader by their linguistic surprises," they develop new power. Stapleton claims, for instance, that "Granite and Steel" is an "example of fresh development in the later poems of Marianne Moore." The poem serves not only as an answer and even a corrective to "the grandiose vision of a voyage to Atlantis in Hart Crane's poem [*The Bridge*]" but also as an affirmation of "the discoveries of the modern mind." It offers "a modern sense of the interacting experience of individuals and a grasp of how an internal vision of the mind can be realized." [10] Stapleton sees Moore's imaginative and poetic strategies as indications of her strength. She believes that Moore continually developed that power, and she marvels at the force of the poems that Moore wrote during the last twenty years of her life.

Helen Vendler takes a thoroughly Olympian approach to Moore and thus has no trace of regret about what Moore chose not to write. Moore's "removal" from "her fellow human beings" becomes not propriety or defense but "superior amusement and denegration."[11] "Marriage" becomes a "satiric comedy," but Moore's poems "remain relatively unpossessed by readers" (72). Vendler points out that "Moore's occasional contempt for the world of male power provokes a counter-attack on what may seem to some her miniature version of life" (74). While far from polemical in their approaches, neither Stapleton nor Vendler were deceived by the disguise in which Moore conducted her own counter-attack on outdated ideas of literature. Thus, their studies complement the groundbreaking contribution of Juhasz and Costello at their own opposite ends of the interpretive continuum. From these studies, one can move on to examine the ways in which Moore seizes, appropriates, and controls the language of the twentieth-century boys' club which she so clearly saw and opposed. Each of these four readings of Marianne Moore, all by women critics, attempts to understand the woman behind the poems. It is curious that the nonpolemical and less scholarly pieces— those by Vendler and Stapleton—are the ones that accept Moore on her own terms and find strength in her self-imposed "limitations." These two studies are, then, the most important steps toward understanding Moore's meticulously designed fictive discourse.

"Sojourn in the Whale," a poem that is anything but modest and deferential, offers more direct insight into the person behind the poems and into the fictive discourse at the core of those poems. The title of the poem is significant in itself since it is the same one Moore gave to her serial account (in letters to her brother) of a trip to New York City in 1915. Determined to succeed as a poet and to meet whoever might help her to achieve that goal, Moore prepared for the task as diligently and deftly as though she were "trying to open locked doors with a sword." (CP, 90). The poem opens with those words, but goes on to show that such impossible tasks seem to accomplish themselves. Power and success follow from essential confidence. The poem is ostensibly addressed to Ireland, whose tasks have included "threading the points of needles" and "planting shade trees upside down." "Swallowed by opaqueness," Ireland has "lived and lived on every kind of shortage" and has "been compelled by hags to spin / gold thread from straw." But Ireland's most impressive qualities are tenacity and inward calm. Speaking directly to Ireland, Moore identifies the secret of that country's power. It is clear that Ireland stands for a person as well as a country:

> [You] have heard men say:
> "There is a feminine temperament in direct contrast to ours,
>
> which makes her do these things. Circumscribed by a
>   heritage of blindness and native

incompetence, she will become wise and will be forced to give in. Compelled by experience, she will turn back;

water seeks its own level":
and you have smiled. "Water in motion is far
from level." You have seen it, when obstacles happened to bar
the path, rise automatically.   (CP, 90)

There is no direct action here, and the poem can thus be read as a gesture of deference. But the smile indicates that the water's power, though hidden, is ferocious. Just as in "The Fish," "water drives a wedge / of iron through the iron edge / of the cliff" (CP, 32). In "Sojourn in the Whale," it rises automatically, fully competent to any challenge.

Moore's image of power asserted by a smile is the keystone in her subversive text and in her fictive discourse as a whole. She has become what Claudine Herrmann calls one of the *voleuses de langue*,[12] one of the thieves of language. Water, particularly, and other images of docility or calm become Moore's codes for subversive discourse, discourse in which the poems often build upon one another.

"Spenser's Ireland," for instance, makes no direct reference to the subject of "Sojourn in the Whale," but it portrays an even more subtle and evasive power. The poem concludes with its speaker's admission that "I am troubled, I'm dissatisfied, I'm Irish," but it has already offered a solution to the alleged dissatisfaction by portraying freedom and success as states of mind rather than as action. We learn, for instance, that dull perseverance which

        again
and again says, "I'll never give in," never sees

that you're not free
    until you've been made captive by
    supreme belief   (CP, 113)

If the eccentricities of Ireland thus seem merely fussy—and Moore's language itself is deliberately fussy when making the point—she has her own suggestion for a method of escape:

                    Erie—
the guillemot
    so neat and the hen
of the heath and the
linnet spinet-sweet—bespeak restlessness? Then

> they are to me
>   like enchanted Earl Gerald who
>   changed himself into a stag, to
> a great green-eyed cat of
> the mountain. Discommodity makes
>   them invisible; they've dis-
> appeared.   (113–114)

"Spenser's Ireland" thus shows that imagination offers escape both from discouragement and, on a whim, from discommodity. The inventiveness of this solution causes the misinterpretations of Moore's fictive discourse that I have been discussing, but identifying the freedom and inventiveness that have always been there offers a corrective to those readings. Moore must be taken on her own terms without looking or wishing for resolutions of grandiose human questions and without assuming that incessant revision indicates weakness and indecision. Approaching Moore on her own terms reveals the ongoing fictive discourse, a dialogue with her contemporaries, and a continuing revelation of self. Moore's discourse does not submit to traditional interpretation, whatever the predilection of her critics, because she plays with the stereotype of feminine passivity and indecision by continually but idiosyncratically asserting her power and control. Moore begins, like her contemporaries, by rejecting and presenting a corrective to the excesses of nineteenth-century romantic verse. She goes on, however, in ways that her contemporaries did not, to question as well the literary tradition preceding it. She rejects the romantic pursuit of capturing and reproducing speech rhythms, even though she admired William Carlos Williams's attempts to do so. She then goes on to question the very efficacy of speech and language. Undoubtedly Marianne Moore intended the resemblance between herself and the subject of "To a Snail"—a creature for whom "modesty is a virtue" and a "curious phenomenon" who recognized the importance of "the incidental [and often ineffable] quality of something well said" (CP, 85). She also resembles the central figure in a later poem entitled "The Student," who refused "to be less // than individual . . . and is too reclusive for / some things to seem to touch / him; not because he / has no feeling but because he has so much" (CP, 102). Those feelings and the curious phenemenon of the way Moore expressed them are the material of Moore's fictive discourse with twentieth-century literature.

Historical Designs

The most obvious characteristic of Moore's fictive discourse is her refusal to be "less than individual." Taken as that unusual whole, the body of Moore's poetry becomes an ongoing conversation with her contemporaries, one that belligerently confronts their beliefs and just as often contradicts her readers' assumptions about poetry. Ezra Pound's *The Cantos* and T. S. Eliot's *The Waste Land,* without doubt the stylistic monoliths of modernism, help to identify Moore's renegade status within the context of high modernism. *The Cantos* and *The Waste Land,* layered with historical references, many of them in the form of quotations, differ markedly from Moore's work even though she participates in the same documentary, allusive, and synthetic method. *The Waste Land* comments on the twentieth century by contrasting sordid contemporary scenes with those of past literary and mythic glory. Unable to accommodate to the sordid present, Eliot's protagonists "drank coffee, and talked for an hour" but did not gain solace from and could not even interpret the "heap of broken images" which loomed in the past as reminders of "that Shakespherian Rag."[13] Like the carbuncular man, "one of the low on whom assurance sits / As a silk hat on a Bradford millionaire" (36), Eliot ranges among images of past glory, but he creates out of them an environment as controlled and devoid of spontaneity as that of *The Waste Land*'s typist. As William Arrowsmith claims, Eliot's use of the past and of quotations either from the words or from the spirit of great texts resembles the technique of the palimpsest. Arrowsmith's essay also shows, however, that Eliot's use of the technique leads invariably to pedantry.[14] While Moore depicts immersion in one's surroundings as a muddy elephant, black earth, sensually acknowledging the "rut upon rut of unpreventable experience" that history has cut into its back, Eliot presents a scene of abstemious frugality and automatic control:

> The typist home at teatime, clears her breakfast, lights
> Her stove, and lays out food in tins.
> Out of the window perilously spread
> Her drying combinations touched by the sun's last rays,
> On the divan are piled (at night her bed)
> Stockings, slippers, camisoles, and stays.   (35–36)

Moore's stance toward literary tradition also differs from Ezra Pound's view of the past. In contrast to Eliot's portrayal of a diminished and unappealing present cowering before past glory, Pound uses history imaginatively but reverentially nonetheless. Pound's heroes range from Odysseus and the ruthless Sigismundo to William Blake and the Confucian wiseman, Kung; but his open-ended search through historical fragments turns out to be circumscribed in its own way as well. Eliot concludes *The Waste Land* with a promise, however tentative, of coming security: "These fragments I have shored against my ruins" (40). Pound demolishes the defensive posture but offers no working substitute:

> These fragments you have shelved (shored),
> "Slut!" "Bitch!" Truth and Calliope
>   Slanging each other *sous les lauriers*[15]

Pound goes on to expose the absurdity of seeking after an ideal or transcendent past:

> . . . the beast with a hundred legs, USURA
> and the swill full of respecters,
>   bowing to the lords of the place,
> explaining its advantages,
>   and the lauditors temporis acti
> claiming that the sh—t used to blacker and richer   (XV, 64)

In the absence of any such resplendent past, these searchers become self-serving as well. They are

> . . . the back-scratchers in a great circle,
>   complaining of insufficient attention,
> the search without end, counterclaim for the missing scratch
> the litigious,
>
> ▪   ▪   ▪   ▪   ▪   ▪   ▪   ▪   ▪   ▪   ▪
>
>   all with twitching backs,
> with daggers, and bottle ends, waiting an
>   unguarded moment   (XV, 64–65)

Thus, although Pound perceives the situation as circular and criticizes the configuration, he also shows that not even as great a prophet as Blake can escape the fate of the back-scratchers. Not even Blake's concerted attempt to escape the vicious circle succeeds:

> And before hell mouth; dry plain
>   and two mountains;
>   On the one mountain, a running form,
>   and another
> In the turn of the hill; in hard steel
> The road like a slow screw's thread,

The angle almost imperceptible,
   so that the circuit seemed hardly to rise;
And the running form, naked, Blake,
Shouting, whirling his arms, the swift limbs
Howling against evil,
   his eyes rolling,
Whirling like flaming cart-wheels,
   and his head held backward to gaze on the evil
As he ran from it,
   to be hid by the steel mountain,
And when he showed again from the north side;
   his eyes blazing toward hell mouth,
His neck forward   (XVI, 68)

Even though Pound's heroes often begin as the countercurrents to their ages, they can neither escape nor significantly alter the age. Thus, in the notes for his latest cantos, Pound's mission has become a search for peace. He cannot, however, conclude that search.

M'amour, m'amour
   what do I love and
      where are you?
That I lost my center
   fighting the world.
The dreams clash
   and are shattered
and that I tried to make a paradiso
                     terrestre.
                  (CXVII, 802)

Pound senses that complacency reproduces itself and mediocrity triumphs. Even Kung, whose wisdom led him to "'respect a child's faculties'" (XIII, 59) and to value "'order'" and "'brotherly deference'" rather than a search for "'life after death,'" knew that ritual offered but a tenuous sense of peace. His warning is clear:

And Kung said, "Without character you will
   be unable to play that instrument
Or to execute the music fit for the Odes.
The blossoms of the apricot
   blow from the east to the west,
And I have tried to keep them from falling."   (XIII, 60)

Perfection is, of course, desirable and character must inform it, but life has its own independent cycles as well. In most cases the blossoms fall and life continues in spite of the loss. Such changes are the material of history. As a result, whether through habit and lethargy, as in *The Waste Land*, or against better judgment and in spite of passionate rage, as in *The Cantos*, the protagonists of modernist poems cannot escape history. Eliot acquiesces and pays homage to it; Pound manipulates and reverses history whenever it suits his purpose. He cannot, however, always control it. Eliot constructs a set of palimpsests in which superimposed layers spark one another and create a whole with powers of its own. Pound's historical fragments litter the present. Instead of the set-piece palimpsest which is Eliot's creation, Pound's is an eye-level voyage through a periplum. In both cases, however, history retains its tarnished identity. It is a foreign presence brought into the text.

The manner in which Pound and Eliot present the fragments that make up these histories emphasizes the way in which they differ from Moore. Pound's voyage takes him through history, apparently without preconceptions, but history cannot be conquered. In Canto II when "men wanting spring-water" land in Scios, they are unable and unwilling to listen to the local boy's warning that their course lies "Not that way!" (7) Each trace of language becomes superimposed and yet retains its own identity. Eliot explains not only that "a good deal of the incidental symbolism of [*The Waste Land*] was suggested by Jessie Weston's *From Ritual to Romance*" but that "Miss Weston's book will elucidate the difficulties of the poem better than my notes can do" (47). Pound includes no such disclaimer and gives no notes to his poems, but the individual identities of its sources rise to the surface with the same insistence as Eliot's do.

Voices from foreign texts play quite a different role in Marianne Moore's poetry, and the introduction to her notes makes the difference clear. While Eliot reverentially pays homage to his chief source and thereby influences his reader's approach to the rest of the notes, Moore offhandedly compares her own notes to "provisos, detainments, and postscripts" and suggests that they be disregarded. Similarly, her quotations recall not the best-known lines from classic works of literature but phrases from everyday life. They are "lines in which the chief interest is borrowed," and they indicate a "hybrid method of composition" (CP, 262) rather than Eliot's erudite "incidental symbolism" of "certain references to vegetation ceremonies" (*Waste Land*, 97).

Moore's ironic attitude toward her quotations thus influences her more comprehensive, alternative approach to and view of the problems and the perceived burden of history. "The Jerboa" shows that the inevitable permutations of history can lead to destructive excesses, but it also offers a simple and convincing escape. The poem begins with an account of how work—commissioned by "A Roman" and executed by "an artist, a freedman"—which had initially "passed / for art" soon became corrupted and overgrown:

A Roman had an
artist, a freedman,
   contrive a cone—a pine-cone
   or a fir-cone—with holes for a fountain.   (CP, 10)

Once in place "on / the Prison of St. Angelo," it "dwarf[s] the peacock / statue in the garden of the Vatican" and, having lost along with proper perspective a sense of its noble origins, seems appropriate only for "a Pompey, or a native / of Thebes." The poem methodically portrays the subtle difference of degree that separates genuine ingenuity from mindless imitation. An "artist, a freedman" "understood making colossi," but his arrogant followers believed in "fantasy / and a verisimilitude that were / right to those with, everywhere, // power over the poor." The difference is almost imperceptible and therefore problematic. The ingenious few who understood making colossi did so presumably because they also understood "how to use slaves." Those who "liked small things" and "gave to boys little paired playthings" also "made toys for them- / selves." Even as ingenuity led toward decorative excess, it kept with it at least a hint of balance, an awareness of its origins:

   Lords and ladies put goose-grease
paint in round bone boxes—the pivoting
lid incised with duck-wing

or reverted duck-
head; kept in a buck
   or rhinoceros horn,
   the ground horn; and locust oil in stone locusts.
     It was a picture with a fine distance;
     of drought, and of assistance

in time, from the Nile
rising slowly   (11)

While ceremony and tradition may keep excess from becoming merely self-serving wastefulness, imitation and decoration are in danger of becoming worthless embarrassments and finally "Too Much." The "evident poetry" of excessive indulgence becomes a bitterly ironic lesson and a false one. What was apparently benevolence becomes abuse:

The bees' food is your
  food. Those who tended flower-
  beds and stables were like the king's cane in the
    form of a hand, or the folding bedroom
    made for his mother of whom

he was fond.   (12)

Fondness aside, the poor, over whom such extravagant rulers have power,
find little that resembles nectar in their own work. Enslaved labor results
instead in false idols—"basalt serpents and portraits of beetles"—or,
even worse, misguided tributes to a ruler's private fears. Maintaining her
supposed impartiality, Moore reveals the king's fear of snakes and portrays his ingenious plan to tame "Pharaoh's rat, the rust- / backed mongoose" to hunt snakes in the palace. Moore admires that tamed animal
for its ability to escape the more comprehensive control that dominates
every other creation of these Roman and Egyptian people. Like the mas-
terful "Nile / rising slowly," which came to the assistance of the self-
absorbed "Lords and ladies," this mongoose succeeds because "its restlessness was its excellence." That directed efficiency becomes Moore's
transition to the poem's real subject, the jerboa.

  [the mongoose] was praised for its wit;
  and the jerboa, like it,

a small desert rat,
and not famous, that
  lives without water, has
  happiness.   (13)

In contrast to all of the other possessions of "Too Much," the jerboa has
no monetary value at all, nor would the jerboa wish for such value. Pre-
ferring "rest and / joy" or "the boundless sand," it is happy with "no
water, no palm-trees, no ivory bed." Moore's reversal and her dismissal
of all that she had earlier presented without judgment is absolute: "one
would not be he / who has nothing but plenty."

Part Two of "The Jerboa," "Abundance," serves as an antidote to "Too
Much" and shows that, while history offers ample evidence of error, corruption, and decay, it also contains happy examples of ingenuity and
perserverance. The jerboa is a model of protective adaption and wise
deference. It "honors the sand by assuming its color," but it also excels
as a model of refinement. It has strength, agility, finesse, and the classic
grace of "a three-cornered smooth-working Chippendale / claw." While
Moore's return to natural history effectively portrays the contrast that is
central to the poem, her design is, as usual, more complex than is at first

apparent. It is true that natural history escapes the corruption attendant upon the mindless pursuit of finery, but Moore also includes an example of corruption reversed, of greed that evolved into success. Within the poem stands Jacob in the midst of flight from the wrath of his brother. Although Jacob had been forgiven and blessed by his father after having stolen one blessing, he eventually recognized that "his friends were the stones" and thus saved himself through ingenuity. The stones formed Jacob's Ladder, "steps of air and angels," and showed him the way to the kingdom that he would eventually establish and rule successfully. Jacob escapes from the consequences of his gullibility, his greed, and his impetuousness; and Moore's treatment of his "Part terrestrial, part celestial" story draws a clear parallel between the poem's two desert dwellers. Merely through choice and authorial design, Moore's Jacob becomes a positive example of the same ingenuity, perseverence, and self-protective instinct that makes the jerboa the hero of the poem. Moore shows that history, even if its source is the Bible, submits itself to fancy. Neither the Bible nor any other great text becomes a burden in Moore's response to the literary tradition she had inherited.

Speech and Writing

The ease with which Marianne Moore turned the burden of literary tradition to her advantage also characterizes the part of her fictive discourse that responds to the challenge of capturing the human voice and recreating its presence in poetry. Moore's approach constitutes another part of her ongoing conversation with her contemporaries. Moore was certainly capable of capturing the subtleties and nuances of the human voice in poetry, but she did so in a way that sets her aside from her contemporaries. Both the differences in those methods and the ramifications of that difference deserve attention.

"A Face," as clearly as any single poem of Moore's, captures tone of voice effectively. It also gives some introduction to the method by which she does so. The poem begins with one of her ubiquitous quotations and continues to develop the deadpan tone of its first two lines:

"I am not treacherous, callous, jealous, superstitious
supercilious, venomous, or absolutely hideous"   (CP, 141)

Related comment, entirely devoid of either self-pity or apology, follows. The speaker possessed of that face studies its expression—"exasperated desperation / though at no real impasse." Whatever the face is expressing, the speaker "would gladly break the glass" that reflects it and escape the situation entirely. The grounds on which Moore wants to make the escape possible are logical but, as she intends, not altogether persuasive:

"Love of order, ardor, uncircuitous simplicity / with an expression of in-quiry, are all one needs to be!" Moore explains her assertion by compar-ing its consequences to a process of attrition. One need remember only certain faces. The speaker progressively alters that to a mere few faces, then to one or two, and finally to one that "to my mind, to my sight, must remain a delight." There are, then, strict qualifications. The face *must* remain a delight, and one can be certain that the remembered one will do so because it, perhaps alone, has survived the process of attrition. The love of order, ardor, simplicity, and inquiry, which dictate the rigor-ous process of selection, also determine the speaker's voice and identity and the personality that makes the selections. The poem's two sentences read like casual, almost colloquial conversation and nearly conceal the artistry of its precise rhyme scheme and syllabic arrangement.

This understatement of Moore's method of presenting human voice stands in direct contrast to William Carlos Williams's continuing search for a line that would capture the subtleties and the fluctuation of speech. Moore insists here and in other poems that the voice be deadpan, that it not seem to convey grand emotions. Instead Moore creates a music par-ticularly suitable for the twentieth century. In such poems as "Marriage" and "Novices" or "To a Snail," "To a Steamroller," and "A Grave," she creates infinitely varying rhythms, complex emotional situations, or vivid personalities. In creating what Justin Replogle has called "tuneful speech," [16] she escapes, however, from the false dilemma of choosing be-tween either a means of recapturing the presence and priority of the spoken voice or an attempt to establish her own written text as superior to her borrowed texts. Williams represents the first attempt, and the final product of Eliot's historic palimpsests represents the other.

Jacques Derrida's refutation of both approaches is strikingly similar to Moore's own method. Derrida builds his critique of Rousseau's *Essay on the Origins of Language* on the claim that in the nostalgic search for the metaphysical presence and priority of spoken language "Rousseau con-siders writing as a dangerous means, a menace, an enterprise of political enslavement." [17] Derrida adds that for Rousseau speech is "natural or at least the natural expression of thought." Writing has been added to speech as a dangerous supplement, and inevitably "the art of writing is nothing but a mediated representation of thought." The process leads to an endless chain of supplements and substitutions that turn writing into a mere "artificial and artful ruse to make speech present when it is actu-ally absent" (144). Derrida goes on to show that Rousseau's concept of writing as secondary, as mere substitution when it "opposes speech to writing as presence to absence and liberty to servitude" (168), becomes "a sort of blind spot" in Rousseau's text (123) and thus a stumbling block. Derrida does not attempt to correct, fill, or erase this blind spot but simply elaborates upon it: "To the extent that [Rousseau] belonged to the metaphysics of presence, he *dreamed* of the simple exteriority of death to life, evil to good, representation to presence, signifier to signified, representer to represented, mask to face, writing to speech. But all such oppositions are irreducibly rooted in that metaphysics" (315).

Just as Moore escapes from the burden of history by manipulating its facts and using them to her own advantage, Derrida regrets Rousseau's continuing participation in traditional metaphysical oppositions and thus does not err by claiming that writing succeeds in replacing that always imagined, that unquestionably pristine origin. Quite the contrary. Derrida wants "to speculate upon the power of exteriority as constitutive of interiority: of speech, of signified meaning, of the present as such" (343). He does not deny that one can trace writing back through speech to an unmediated human cry. Rather he adds to that assumption one which he delights in knowing will be "totally unacceptable as it is within classical logic" (313). Having demolished the attempt to recapture speech as an ultimate goal, Derrida proposes a solution that is as unresolved as Moore's epigrammatic closings. The problem is not a problem after all. "One can no longer see disease in substitution when one sees that the substitute is substituted for a substitute" (314).

The precarious balance that Derrida wants to establish refuses to grant absolute priority either to speech or to the writing which replaces it. Moore's poems establish the same balance. Her quotations represent voices different from her own, but they do not attempt to mimic those voices and make them present within the text. By insisting upon the separate existence of her quotations and of the objects she includes in her poems, Moore creates new objects, poems that have been called collages. If they are collages, they have been assembled with rubber glue rather than with permanent cement. Moore reserves the right to unmake her poems, but she insists that each version of a poem remain visible. Like Derrida, who appropriated Freud's mystic writing pad, Moore puts both the speech and the objects in her poems under erasure.

"Poetry," with its three-line version offered in the main text and its original not really suppressed but removed to the "Notes," is the most obvious example. The process is more subtle in "The Steeple-Jack." The poem first appeared in the June 1932 issue of *Poetry*, along with "The Hero" and "The Student," under the collective title "Part of a Novel, Part of a Poem, Part of a Play." Two years later, in *Selected Poems*, it appeared under the same title, but "The Student" was missing from the trio. Moore had made several alterations in "The Steeple-Jack," and she entered even more corrections in presentation copies of *Selected Poems*. In *Collected Poems*, she removed the tripartite title as well as five stanzas of "The Steeple-Jack" and half of two others. The new, broken poem stands as testament to its earlier integrity, and the partial stanzas call attention to their missing parts. In *Complete Poems*, Moore restores those stanzas, and the poem resembles but doesn't quite duplicate its original form. Having been kept out of *Collected Poems* and *A Marianne Moore Reader*, "The Student" reappears as it did in *What Are Years* (1941), vastly altered from its 1932 *Poetry* version. "An Octopus" suffered excisions also. By 1955, in *Collected Poems*, it had lost 32 lines that describe the rich sea of colored flowers covering the "treacherous glassy mountain" and "the blue Jay" who wisely

> knows no Greek,
> 'that pride-producing language',
> in which 'rashness is rendered innocuous, and error exposed
> by the collision of knowledge with knowledge'.   (SP, 87)

The error of a "pride-producing language" is believing that it is inviolable, and Moore corrects that error by her rashness in revising. Just as Moore used quotations and created human voices to undermine rather than to restore the priority of speech, she also denies the integrity of her own written texts. Poems such as "Poetry," "The Steeple-Jack," and "The Octopus" make this clear, but they also raise questions about the wisdom of her practice and invite charges of indecision or mere fussiness. In fact, some of Moore's changes weaken her poems by diminishing the force of her irony or taming the best effects of her verbal excess. Other changes seem the result of overly scrupulous tampering. Moore even continued to alter some poems after she published them so that certain changes appear only in presentation copies of her books.

With typical assurance, however, Moore answers those charges and offers another interpretation of her actions. She does so most clearly in "Peter," where her ostensible subject is a cat. Moore appears merely to be describing feline behavior, but she also argues for her absólute right, even her obligation, to manipulate printed texts. "Strong and slippery, / built for a midnight grass-party," the cat named Peter seems the picture of passivity and malleability:

> He lets himself be flattened out by gravity,
> as seaweed is tamed and weakened by the sun,
> compelled when extended, to lie stationary. (CP, 43)

Sleep, though, is a mere delusion—both for Peter, who believes sleep to be the "epitome of what is to him the end of life," and for the lady who teases and wakens him. She finds beneath Peter's deceptively passive exterior an independent and potentially combative spirit. The double perspective is essential to Moore's argument. For Peter to deny either part of himself would be hypocrisy. He can abandon a toy "when it shows signs of being no longer a pleasure." More to the point, he can extend "the detached first claw . . . retracted to its tip" and "score the nearby magazine with a double line of strokes." Peter does not need to apologize for such behavior. "When one is frank, one's very presence is a compliment."

Moore exploits this self-assured double perspective throughout her poetry. She is outwardly as docile as Peter seems to be, but she has another side as well. Her docility is not "a fixed illusion." If one argues against "the disposition invariably to affront," Moore answers that "an animal with claws should have an opportunity to use them" (44). Moore's solution reveals the creative freedom she values:

> To leap, to lengthen out, divide the air, to purloin, to pursue.
> To tell the hen: fly over the fence, go in the wrong way
> in your perturbation—this is life;
> to do less would be nothing but dishonesty. (44)

Helen Vendler calls this "superior amusement and denegration . . . the source of [Moore's] virgin strength" (*Part of Nature*, 67). The strength comes from Moore's plays on and within the forms of indecision and from her ironic mask of feminity. Although Moore frequently speaks without an artificial mask—in poems such as "Marriage," "A Grave," "The Paper Nautilus," and "Nevertheless"—the technique of the mask of assumed innocence and docility works effectively when she does employ it.

In "To a Giraffe," for instance, the speaker is apparently unaware of the irony of the towering animal who solves the ban against being "personal" by living "only on the top leaves that are small" and by being "unconversational." "Plagued by the psychological," such a creature can be "unbearable," but he is also mercifully "less conversational" than "some emotionally-tied-in-knots animal." While speechlessness seems to be a workable solution, Moore's conclusion undercuts that assurance by turning toward paradigmatic speech—philosophical speculation. Perfect solutions do not exist.

> After all
> consolations of the metaphysical
> can be profound. In Homer, existence
>
> is flawed; transcendence, conditional;
> "the journey from sin to redemption, perpetual." (CP, 215)

"Values in Use" also questions but does not dismiss the possibility of gaining knowledge through language. The poem's speaker "attended school" and "liked the place," but never understood the urgency of the challenge to " 'create / values in the process of living'" rather than " 'await their historic progress.'" The speaker thus remains "still abstruse." Ironically, a puzzled student's "offhand" comment makes his own perhaps unorthodox sense of the various classroom conversations in which "writing was discussed":

" 'Relevant' and 'plausible' were words I understand."

A pleasing statement, anonymous friend.
Certainly the means must not defeat the end.   (CP, 181)

Academic concerns may complicate more issues than they simplify, and pretentious conversations should not be tolerated. Nevertheless, words in their purest form still have value and power. "To a Giraffe" marks a clear change from Moore's tone of easy dismissal in such well-known early poems as "To a Snail" or "To a Steamroller" to her later, less imperative one in "Dream" or "Values in Use." There is, however, a continuity in the identity she assumes. Moore is a fearless speaker who will tolerate nothing but truth, and she respects or manipulates language according to those priorities. Thus, just as Moore used literary tradition to her own purposes and refused to be burdened by it, she approached human speech and all language as tools to employ in her poetry whenever it was convenient. She felt no need to privilege unwritten speech, but she also insisted that written texts and great ideas were unpredictable and subject to change.

"Words and . . ." a Smile

Moore's refusal to privilege either the spoken language behind writing or the written line itself leads to a question about the identity of the person who wrote the poems. Those imaginary portraits range from what Helen Vendler describes as "the silent well-brought-up-girl who thinks up mute rejoinders during every parlor conversation" (*Part of Nature*, 63) to the emotionally overwhelmed but strong-minded speaker of "Marriage" and from the whimsical dreamer of "A Carriage Made in Sweden" and "O To Be a Dragon" to the somber thinker of "In Distrust of Merits." At her most enchanting and optimistic, Moore imagines the clear, sweet air of Sweden where the cart that she now admires in Brooklyn was made. She infuses that fantasy with the stubborn feminine temperament that the detractors of "Sojourn in the Whale" mistakenly predicted would result in submissive defeat. The "flowered step swan- / dart brake, and swirling crustacean- / tailed equine amphibious creatures / that garnish the axle tree" (131) of the carriage inspire the poet's mind's eye to imagine in equally vivid detail Sweden's "Sun-right gable- / ends due east and west, the table / spread as for a banquet; and the put- / in twin vest-pleats with a fish-fin // effect when you need none" (CP, 132).

Although Moore deliberately creates the image of an impressionable, romantic speaker in "A Carriage Made in Sweden," she takes that appreciation for fine detail a step further in "An Arctic Ox." The poem equates imagined finery, in this case clothing—"a suit of / *quiviut,* so light I did not / know I had it on; and in the / course of time, another"—with the animals that produce the wool, those choice pets with disarmingly human characteristics. Their distinction, Moore insists, is "not egocentric scent" but intelligence, and she pays homage both to the animals and to the products they make possible. Moore wants a suit of *quiviut.* It would be "so light I did not / know I had it on" (193), and she can have it without harming the animal. This observation opens the poem:

> To wear the arctic fox
> you have to kill it. Wear
>   *quiviut*—the underwool of the arctic ox—
> pulled off it like a sweater;
> your coat is warm; your conscience, better.   (CP, 193)

The poem goes on to combine scientific fact and observation with imaginative fancy in order to defend the animal and persuade others to do the same. They are "not incapable / of courtship," but

>   may find its
>   servitude and flutter, too much
> like Procrustes' bed;
> some decide to stay unwed.   (CP, 194)

While this removal from courtship certainly resembles Moore herself and may account for her fanciful interest in the animal, the animals have other endearing, human qualities as well:

> They join you as you work;
> love jumping in and out of holes,
>   play in water with their children,
> learn fast, know their names,
> will open gates and invent games.   (194)

At the whim of this imaginative speaker, the poem meanders about, creating out of the wool "a twenty-four-or-five- / mile thread—one forty-ply— / that will not shrink in any dye" (195).

But the poem then ends abruptly with a return to more sensible concerns:

If you fear that you are
reading an advertisement,
        you are. If we can't be cordial
to these creatures' fleece,
I think that we deserve to freeze.   (195)

The speaker seems to be as inconstant as she is imaginative, and the freedom that informs her contrasting moods stands at the core of all of
Moore's speakers. They refuse to follow the rules and make the assumptions of her contemporaries, and the poems in which they speak carry
Moore's signature.

It has been difficult to perceive the various pieces of her design as a
coherent whole, but, as we approach the one hundredth anniversary of
Moore's birth, we can with the wisdom of hindsight begin to form a picture of the woman behind her words. Moore entered the dialogue of her
contemporaries when it concerned the ways in which a writer might
confront the burden of living in the twentieth century, but she treated
that burden as a challenge, a game. In response to the inevitable search
for a new form appropriate to that age, Moore invented a style and a
language so individual that it has become inseparable from later perceptions of the person who created the style. She herself insisted, by means
of constant revisions and restorations, that the person behind the poems
was more important and would continue to be more important than either metaphysical truth or a set poem as artifact.

In Moore's case, however, the person behind the words is difficult to
capture. Beyond their surface difficulty, Moore's poems present a self-
portrait, a gradually emerging speaker, but not in any of the senses traditionally known as autobiography. They tell a tale of gradual growth
and change and of a continually developing love of words, one that un-
derlies and affects her treatment of any subject or emotion whatsoever. It
is difficult work, certainly. But in spite of Moore's well-publicized and
properly docile disclaimers, the challenges and puzzles pleased Moore
thoroughly.

In 1961, when Moore was seventy-four years old, she wrote a forward
to *A Marianne Moore Reader,* which is as witty, as deliberately strange,
and as quietly contradictory and arrogant as anything she ever wrote; it
serves now as a clue to the degree to which Moore wished to be open
and direct, but only for those willing to enter her curious frame of reference. Moore begins the forward by outlining the supposed reasons for
reissuing her work in such a highly selective edition, but she goes on to
ridicule the impulse and call it into question. Eventually Moore answers
her own objections with the smile of the feminine temperament of "Sojourn in the Whale":

Published: it is enough. The magazine was discontinued. The edition was small. One paragraph needs restating. Newpaper cuts on the fold and disintegrates. When was it published and where? "The title was 'Words and . . .' something else. Could you say what it was?" I have forgotten. Happened upon years later, it seems to have been "Words and Modes of Expression." What became of "Tedium and Integrity," the unfinished manuscript of which there was no duplicate? A housekeeper is needed to assort the untidiness. For whom? A curioso or just for the author? In that case "as safe at the publisher's as if chained to shelves of Bodley," Lamb said, smiling.[18]

Safe as it may be at the publishers, both the work and its principles of selection face questions and objections when it reaches its public. Moore answers these in the next paragraph of her forward. This time her rhetorical questions leave no doubt as to how they should be answered:

Verse: prose: a specimen or so of translation for those on whom completeness would weigh as a leg-iron. How would it seem to me if someone else had written it? Does it hold the attention? "Has it human values?" Or seem as if one had ever heard of "lucidity, force, and ease" or had any help from past thinkers? Is it subservient sing-song or has it "muscles"? (xiii)

Moore's work does have that muscle. It constructed the disguises, the masks of her poems, and it is part of more than the form of those poems. Moore's muscle pervades every emotion that she portrays, whether experienced or observed. It insists that the American landscape and the American speech that she loved were a challenge for the strong. Most of all, Moore's muscle enjoys showing the power that a solitary feminine speaker can harness. Whether as an idle browser in a museum or curio shop, an explorer on a glacial mountain, a purchaser of fine clothing, or a fantastic dreamer, the feminine voice that Moore invents and perpetuates is a forceful one. It develops from the already secure knowledge that "dislike" and "contempt" soon fade before the "genuine," and it finds itself able to rise above "insolence and triviality" in favor of the "raw material of poetry." The muscle knows, as Moore puts it in "People's Surroundings," that "one's style is not lost in such simplicity." There is "something attractive about a mind that moves in a straight line." One learns to be an observer par excellence so that "the eye knows what to skip; . . . with X-ray-like inquisitive intensity upon it, the surfaces go back" (CP, 57). Fundamental structure emerges. Moore shows us how to develop that X-ray-like inquisitive intensity and shows us, too, the joy of such vision. Moore's vision, like that of "The Student," knows that "refusing to be less // than individual" offers only the dull escape of "bookworms, mildews, / and complaisancies" (CP, 102).

The individual muscle of Moore's curious poems and of the curious mind that made them cannot be contained within a grand system such as Yeats's poetic self-monument. Nor does it address the concerns of the twentieth century on the grandiose scales of Pound, Eliot, Stevens, and Williams. Although Moore carefully alters Biblical tales and classical mythology to suit her own purposes, her random changes hardly approach the methodical interpretation that Alicia Ostriker has identified in H.D.'s poetry.[19] In choosing, however, to remain a "student," Moore never abandons the muscle. She insists, nonetheless, that the muscle is a feminine one. Not only has she not joined the boy's club, she has created a private and most interesting haven of her own. Like her student, Moore writes in solitude and gives her opinion, but never troubles to defend it. She "renders service when there is / no reward," and seems reclusive not because she "has no feeling but because [s]he has so much" (CP, 102). Moore controlled her words and her poems in a manner that forbade them to become defensively ironic and closed. In the process of writing them, then, she showed that the feminine temperament of the poems controlled their freedom absolutely. The task of creation is the subject of Moore's poems. It is a fictive discourse of constant observation, of growth, and of imagination. Like the student's scientific experiment, the process of creating poems " 'is never finished.'" Nor is the challenge of reading the poems and recognizing both the feminity and the muscularity of that discourse.

A comment that Moore made about Emily Dickinson in her review of the 1931 edition of Dickinson's letters suggests what Moore might have said about her own work and its public reception as well as about how she might more profitably be read. Moore had read and admired the new edition of Dickinson's letters, but even more she admired Mabel Loomis Todd's decision to let the letters speak for themselves before " 'so enabled a man' as the twentieth-century critic"[20] might create his own version of Emily Dickinson. The collection presented, Moore thought, a "wholly non-notorious personality, an absence of legend" (220). More importantly, it offered insight into Dickinson's process of composition: "If we care about the poems, we value the connection in which certain poems and sayings originated" (221). The lesson was an important one since Dickinson was undoubtedly the most important American woman poet who had preceded Moore and since Moore was a dutiful but not uncritical student of the poetry of others. Thus she challenged the commentators who accused Dickinson of vanity to read the poet more carefully and with a more open mind: "A sense of drama with which we may not be quite at home—was for her a part of that expansion of breath necessary to existence, and unless it is conceited for the hummingbird or the osprey to not behave like a chicken, one does not find her conceited" (225).

As though able to predict the ways in which a new generation of critics would dismiss or misperceive her own poetry, Moore added a comment about Dickinson that applies today to Moore as well: "She was not a recluse, nor was her work, in her thought of it, something eternally sealed." Dickinson was, instead, "that rare thing, the truly unartificial spirit—flashing like an animal, with strength or dismay." Moore "resents" those who ask why "Emily Dickinson should sit in the dim hall to listen to Mrs. Todd's music." For Moore, that practice becomes an enabling metaphor for ongoing individual creation. It also serves as a hopeful prediction for the reception and understanding of Moore's work: "Music coming from under a window has many times been enhanced by its separateness; and though to converse athwart a door is not usual, it seems more un-useful to discuss such a preference than it would be to analyze the beam of light that brings personality, even in death, out of seclusion" (222).

Notes

1. Portrait of a Writing Master

1. Marianne Moore, *Complete Poems* (New York: Macmillan, 1981), 119. All quotations from Moore's poetry, unless otherwise indicated, will be from this edition, subsequently abbreviated CP.

2. Conversation with Kenneth Burke, April 23, 1982.

3. R. P. Blackmur, "A Critic's Job of Work," in *Language as Gesture* (London: George Allen and Unwin, 1961), 397.

4. R. P. Blackmur, "The Method of Marianne Moore," in *Marianne Moore: A Collection of Critical Essays,* ed. Charles Tomlinson (Englewood Cliffs, N.J.: Prentice Hall, 1969), 66.

5. John Crowe Ransom, "On Being Modern with Distinction," *Quarterly Review of Literature* 4, 2 (1948): 136.

6. Roy Harvey Pearce, *The Continuity of American Poetry* (Princeton, N.J.: Princeton University Press, 1961), 369.

7. Hugh Kenner, "Meditation and Enactment," in *Marianne Moore: A Collection of Critical Essays,* ed. Charles Tomlinson (Englewood Cliffs, N.J.: Prentice Hall, 1969), 161.

8. George W. Nitchie, *Marianne Moore: An Introduction to the Poetry* (New York: Columbia University Press, 1969), 173–174.

9. Pamela White Hadas, *Marianne Moore: Poet of Affection* (Syracuse, N.Y.: Syracuse University Press, 1977), 103.

10. Hugh Kenner, *Homemade World: The American Modernist Writers* (New York: Alfred A. Knopf, 1975), xviii.

11. Mary Warner Moore to Marianne Moore, 19 November 1908. Unless otherwise indicated, all letters are from the Marianne Moore archives of the Rosenbach Foundation Museum and Library.

12. Marianne Moore to Mary Warner Moore, 15 November 1915.

13. Marianne Moore to John Warner Moore, 26 November 1915.

14. Marianne Moore to John Warner Moore, 15 December, 19 December, and 22 December, 1915.

15. Marianne Moore in a note added to a letter by Mary Warner Moore to John Warner Moore, 15 December 1915.

16. Marianne Moore to H. D., 10 November 1916.

17. William Carlos Williams to Marianne Moore, 16 November 1919, and Marianne Moore to William Carlos Williams, on verso.

18. Alfred Kreymborg, *Troubadour: An American Biography* (New York: Sagamore Press, 1957), 186–187.

19. Robert McAlmon, *Post Adolescence* (Paris: Contact Publishing Company, n.d.) 18.

20. Robert McAlmon to Marianne Moore, 12 April 1921.

21. Marianne Moore to Robert McAlmon, 18 June 1921.

22. Marianne Moore to Bryher, 31 August 1921.

23. Marianne Moore, "Letter to Barbara Kurz," *Marianne Moore Newsletter* 1, no. 2 (Fall 1977): 7.

24. Marianne Moore, *Collected Poems* (New York: Macmillan, 1951), 47. Subsequent quotations from "Melancthon" will be from this edition, abbreviated ColP.

2. Compact, Subtle Essays

1. See Patricia Willis, "No Swan So Fine," *Marianne Moore Newsletter* 2, no. 1 (Spring 1978): 2–5, for a full account of Moore's composition of the poem.

2. William Butler Yeats, "Sailing to Byzantium," *Collected Poems* (New York: Macmillan, 1973), 192.

3. The essays I have examined for this chapter include all the signed essays and reviews Moore published before editing *The Dial*, the unsigned "Briefer Mentions" she published both before her editorship and during it, and the few signed reviews she published in *The Dial* while she was editor. "Comment," the official editorial column she wrote each month while editor, will be treated by itself in Chapter 3.

4. Kenner, *Homemade World*, 101.

5. Donald Hall, *Marianne Moore: The Cage and the Animal* (New York: Pegasus, 1970), 136.

6. Bernard Engel, *Marianne Moore* (New York: Twayne, 1961), 129.

7. Kenneth Burke, "Likings of an Observationist," in *Marianne Moore*, ed. Charles Tomlinson (Englewood Cliffs, N.J.: Prentice Hall, 1969), 126–127.

8. Marianne Moore, "Samuel Butler," *Chimaera* 1 (July 1916): 55–58.

9. The typescript is in the Marianne Moore archives at the Rosenbach Foundation Museum. Since Moore did not note the deletion on her own copy of the manuscript, as was her usual practice, the cut was presumably made by Harriet Shaw Weaver at *The Egoist*.

10. Marianne Moore, "The Accented Syllable," *The Egoist* 3 (October 1916): 151–152.

11. Marianne Moore, "A Note on T. S. Eliot's Book," *Poetry* 12 (April 1918): 36–37.

12. Marianne Moore, "Is the Real Actual?" *The Dial* 73 (December 1922): 620–622.

13. Marianne Moore, "Well Moused, Lion," *The Dial* 76 (June 1924): 84–91.

14. Marianne Moore, "The Spare American Emotion," *The Dial* 80 (February 1926): 153–156.

3. *The Dial* as "Aesthetic Equivalent"

1. Frederick Hoffman, Charles Allen, and Carolyn Ulrich's *The Little Magazine* (Princeton, N.J.: Princeton University Press, 1946) devotes a chapter to *The Dial*. William Wasserstrom's *The Time of* The Dial (Syracuse: Syracuse University Press, 1963) takes a broad view of the magazine, and Nicolas Joost's *Scofield Thayer and* The Dial (Carbondale: Southern Illinois University Press, 1964) necessarily concentrates on the years during which Thayer acted as the magazine's editor.

2. T. S. Eliot, "Ulysses, Order annd Myth," *Selected Prose of T. S. Eliot* (New York: Harcourt, Brace Jovanovich, 1975), 177.

3. John Crowe Ransom, "On Being Modern with Distinction," *Quarterly Review of Literature* 4, no. 2 (1948): 136.

4. Wasserstrom, *The Time of* The Dial, 110.

5. Scofield Thayer, "Comment," *The Dial* 75 (October 1923): 402.

6. Joost, *Scofield Thayer and* The Dial, 122.

7. Jacques Lacan, *Ecrits: A Selection,* trans. Alan Sheridan (New York: New Directions, 1971), 6.

8. Marianne Moore, "Announcement," *The Dial* 86 (January 1929): 90.

9. From the entry on 27 April 1925 in Moore's appointment notebook, Marianne Moore archives, Rosenbach Foundation Museum. Although Moore's name first appears as acting editor for the July 1925 issue and as editor in July 1926, *The Dial* correspondence in the Beinecke Library indicates that her official connection with the magazine began even earlier. A note to Moore from Alyse Gregory, managing editor for *The Dial,* written on 26 February 1924, invites Moore to attend the magazine's make-up meeting so that she would be able to write the monthly clipsheet, an advertising brochure circulated in advance of each issue.

10. Scofield Thayer to Ezra Pound, 23 April 1923. All subsequent references to unpublished correspondence are to material in *The Dial* archives at the Beinecke Library.

11. Ezra Pound to Marianne Moore, 12 January and 9 February 1927.

12. J. Sibley Watson to Marianne Moore, 27 February 1927.

13. J. Sibley Watson to Ezra Pound, 19 October 1927.

14. Charles K. Trueblood, "Biography," *The Dial* 83 (August 1927): 130.

15. William Carlos Williams, "The Venus," *The Dial* 85 (July 1928): 21.

16. William Carlos Williams, "Marianne Moore," *Selected Essays of William Carlos Williams* (New York: New Directions, 1954), 121.

17. In referring to Moore's "Comments" I will use that title rather than the two or three titles Craig Abbot attributes to them in his *Marianne Moore: A Descriptive Bibliography* (Pittsburgh: University of Pittsburgh Press, 1977). Subsequent references to *Dial* pieces will appear parenthetically by volume, date, and page number.

18. Longinus, "On the Sublime," in *Critical Theory Since Plato,* ed. Hazard Adams (New York: Harcourt, Brace Jovanovich, 1971), 83.

19. Edward Said, *Beginnings: Intention and Method* (New York: Basic Books, 1975), 292.

20. Marianne Moore, "New York," *Complete Poems*, 54. The poem first appeared in *The Dial* (71, December 1921).

21. Moore borrowed the phrase "accessibility to experience" from James. In "Henry James as a Characteristic American," *Predilections* (New York: Viking Press, 1955), 21–31, Moore writes that "If good-nature and reciprocity are American traits, Henry James was a characteristic American." Even more to the point she quotes James's own claim that a characteristic American would be "'intrinsically and actively ample . . . reaching westward, southward, anywhere, everywhere,' with a mind 'incapable of the shut door in any direction'" (31). The essay first appeared in *Hound and Horn* 7 (April–May 1934): 361–372.

22. Frederic Jameson, *The Political Unconscious: Narrative as a Socially Symbolic Act* (New York: Cornell University Press, 1981), 9.

4. "A Reality of Her Own Particulars"

1. Charles Olson, "Letter 3," *Selected Writings*, ed. Robert Creeley (New York: New Directions, 1960), 226.

2. J. Hillis Miller, "The Critic as Host," *Critical Inquiry* 3 (Spring 1977): 442 and 444.

3. In "The Critic as Host," Miller begins by asking "can host and parasite live happily together, in the domicile of the same text, feeding each other and sharing the food?" Miller's elaborate and amusing reconstruction of the meanings and possible meanings of "parasite" and "host," about which he dutifully warns, "I have only begun to go as far I mean to go," leads him to conclude that the relationship between a critic and the text he hosts, while not symbiotic, cannot be reduced to its simplistic "opposite." In this schema, a critic and his text are

fellow guests "beside the grain," host and guest, host and host, host and parasite, parasite and parasite. The relationship is a triangle, not a polar opposition. There is always a third to whom the two are related, something before them or between them, which they divide, consume, or exchange, across which they meet. Or rather, the relation in question is always a chain, that strange sort of chain without beginning or end in which no commanding element (origin, goal, or underlying principle) may be identified, but in which there is always something earlier or something later to which any part of the chain on which one focuses refers and which keeps the chain open, undecidable. The relation between any two contiguous elements in this chain is that strange opposition which is of intimate kinship and at the same time of enmity. It is therefore not able to be encompassed in the ordinary logic of polar opposition, nor is it open to dialectal synthesis. (444)

I use the metaphor in Miller's sense. Moore is both the perfect guest who accommodates herself to the needs of her host and her own unassimilated self as well.

4. Marjorie Perloff, *The Poetics of Indeterminacy* (Princeton: Princeton University Press, 1981).

5. Frank Lentricchia, *After the New Criticism* (Chicago: University of Chicago Press, 1980), xiv.

6. Wallace Stevens, "About One of Marianne Moore's Poems," *The Necessary Angel: Essays on Reality and the Imagination* (New York: Vintage Books, 1951), 95.

Subsequent quotations from this essay as well as "Effects of Analogy," "Imagination as Value," "The Noble Rider and the Sound of Words," and "Three Academic Pieces" are taken from this edition.

7. Marianne Moore, "Things Others Never Notice," *Predilections* (New York: Viking Press, 1955), 137. Subsequent quotations from this essay as well as from "Conjuries That Endure," "Feeling and Precision," "Humility, Concentration, and Gusto," "There is a War That Never Ends," "Things Others Never Notice," and "*The Dial* Award" are from this edition, abbreviated Pred.

8. Geoffrey Hartman, *Criticism in the Wilderness* (New Haven: Yale University Press, 1980), 119.

9. Denise Levertov, "Great Possessions," *The Poet in the World* (New York: New Directions, 1973), 90.

10. William Carlos Williams, "Prologue to *Kora in Hell*," in *Selected Essays of William Carlos Williams* (New York: New Directions, 1954), 20–21. Subsequent quotations from this essay as well as "Marianne Moore" are from this edition.

11. William Carlos Williams, *Collected Early Poems* (New York: New Directions, 1966), 249.

12. William Carlos Williams, "The Descent of Winter," *Imaginations* (New York: New Directions, 1970), 238–239.

13. William Carlos Williams, *Selected Poems* (New York: New Directions, 1969), 152.

14. Denise Levertov, "A Note on the Work of the Imagination," *The Poet in the World*, 205.

5. Craftsmanship Disfigured and Restored

1. Paul de Man, "Shelly Disfigured," *Deconstruction and Criticism* (New York: Seabury Press, 1979), 69.

2. Barbara Herrnstein Smith, *Poetic Closure: A Study of How Poems End* (Chicago: University of Chicago Press, 1968), 237.

3. Marianne Moore, "Poetry," *Observations* (New York: Dial Press, 1925). 31.

6. "And You Have Smiled"

1. Moore, *Complete Poems*, 267. As discussed in the preceding chapter, Moore included the earlier version of "Poetry" in the notes to *Complete Poems*. The list that Moore offers to illustrate such entities includes such a variety of subjects that their only unifying characteristic seems to be inscrutability. They range from "the bat / holding on upside down or in quest of something to // eat, elephants pushing, a wild horse taking a roll, a tireless wolf under / a tree, the immovable critic twitching his skin like a horse that feels a flea, the base- / ball fan, the statistician," to " 'business documents and school-books.' "

2. Elaine Showalter, "Feminist Criticism in the Wilderness," *Critical Inquiry* 8, no. 2 (Winter 1981): 180.

3. Barbara Herrnstein Smith, *On the Margins of Discourse* (Chicago: University of Chicago Press, 1978), 39.

4. Friedrich Nietzsche, *The Gay Science* in *A Nietzsche Reader*, ed. R. J. Hollingdale (New York: Penguin Books, 1977), 66.

5. Edith Hamilton, *Mythology: Timeless Tales of Gods and Heroes* (New York: Mentor Books, 1969), 63.

6. Suzanne Juhasz, "'Felicitous Phenomenon': The Poetry of Marianne Moore," in *Naked and Fiery Forms: Modern American Poetry by Women* (New York: Octagon Books, 1976), 37.

7. Elaine Showalter, "Comments on Jehlin's 'Archimedes and the Paradox of Feminist Criticism,'" *Signs* 8, no. 1 (Autumn 1982): 162.

8. Alicia Ostriker, "The Thieves of Language: Women Poets and Revisionist Mythmaking," *Signs* 8, no. 1 (Autumn 1982): 69.

9. Bonnie Costello, *Marianne Moore: Imaginary Possessions* (Cambridge, Harvard University Press, 1981), 182.

10. Laurence Stapleton, *Marianne Moore: The Poet's Advance* (Princeton: Princeton University Press, 1978), 209–210.

11. Helen Vendler, "Marianne Moore," in *Part of Nature, Part of Us* (Cambridge: Harvard University Press, 1980), 67.

12. Claudine Herrmann, *Les Voleuses de Langue* (Paris: Des Femmes, 1979). Quoted in Ostriker, "The Thieves of Language," *Signs* 8, no. 1 (Autumn 1982): 69.

13. T. S. Eliot, *The Waste Land and Other Poems* (London: Faber and Faber, 1973) 27, 31. Subsequent references are to this edition.

14. William Arrowsmith, "Eros in Terre Haute: T. S. Eliot's 'Lune de Miel,'" *The New Criterion* 1, no. 2 (October 1982): 27. Arrowsmith's imaginary conversation inevitably and ironically turns into a battle of academic one-upmanship.

15. Ezra Pound, *The Cantos* (New York: New Directions, 1972), VIII, 28. Subsequent references are to this edition.

16. Justin Replogle, "Marianne Moore and the Art of Intonation," *Contemporary Literature*, 12, no. 1 (Autumn 1971): 17.

17. Jacques Derrida, *Of Grammatology* (Baltimore: Johns Hopkins, 1976), 301.

18. Marianne Moore, *A Marianne Moore Reader* (New York: The Viking Press, 1961), xiii.

19. Alicia Ostriker, "Learning to Read H. D." *American Poetry Review* 12, no. 2 (March–April 1983): 29–38.

20. Marianne Moore, "Emily Dickinson," *Poetry* 41 (January 1933): 220.

Index